Josh and Tilly's Adventures

In Ripon Cathedral

Contributors

…ors: Arlene Coulson, Lynne Ditchburn, Helen Entwisle, Kath Hall, …y Hallett, Carol Priestley, Joseph Priestley, Carolyn Sands, Moira …ker, Dorothy Taylor, Louise Watson.

…ustrations, identified by following initials: Jen Deadman (JD), Helen …twisle (HE), Anne Groves (AG), Phoebe Hall (PH), Jennifer Hardisty …I), Unity Hield (UH), David Mayoh (DM), Rose Priestley (RP), Dorothy …ylor (DT), Lesley Taylor (LT).

…ol involvement: the pupils of Cathedral C of E Primary School, …tone Community Primary School, Holy Trinity C of E Junior School …t. Wilfrid's Catholic Primary School provided artwork and stories.

Photos: Ian Stalker, unless otherwise accredited.

Proofreaders: Gillian Brackenbury, Sue Ford, Malcolm Hanson.

Compilation and design: Ian Stalker.

Editor: Toria Forsyth-Moser.

Painting on front cover by Ryan Glass
Illuminated initials: Dorothy Taylor

Contents

Chapter 1

The Celtic Cross

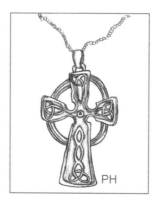

Tilly and Josh, inseparable twins aged ten and three quarters, were wandering off down a side aisle of the Cathedral, whilst their Mum was busy talking to the Welcomer in the red gown at the main door. The twins were examining the pictures embroidered into the cushions all around the wall ledges, when something caught Tilly's eye.

'Look,' she whispered. 'There's a stone floor slab out of place down here in this corner, where men were working on the wiring for the new lighting. I wonder if there is anything exciting underneath?' She looked around to see whether anyone was watching and no one was. She also noticed that her Mum had gone into the shop, probably to buy a birthday card for their Dad. She would be simply ages choosing that.

'Let's see if we can see underneath. I think there is just room to squeeze in. Come on Josh!' They lowered themselves carefully into the narrow space and found it widened out a bit, if you crouched down. They got down on all fours and discovered there was an old chest on its side, half buried in rubble, but the lid was gaping open slightly and an eerie glow came through the slit. They managed to drag it back towards them, so that they could sit on the edges of the hole.

'Ooh, it's just waiting for us to explore', said Tilly. 'Help me pull the lid up a bit further Josh.' They tugged and tugged at the lid, until it creaked open just enough for them to see that the box was not empty. Josh warily put his hand in and felt around. He caught the cold hard edge of something and worked it loose from the tangle of stuff around it. It was a small cross attached to a chain, but this cross was different – it had a circle joining the arms. They both stroked the smooth metal gently and something very peculiar began to happen, as though they had touched a memory…

'Why is the sun suddenly shining in here?' asked Josh.

'It's not', Tilly replied. 'We are outside and what's more we are dressed in peculiar clothes. Just look at yourself! You have a tunic and a cap and I'm in a long pinafore dress and my hair is in braids!'

'Cool!' exclaimed Josh. 'I think we are time travelling like Dr Who. We must have gone back to a time before the Cathedral was built. We are standing outside because there was nothing on this spot then. There are some wooden buildings with thatched roofs and gardens round them, just over there,' he pointed, 'and there's a big stone cross like this small one we're holding.'

'Wow!' whispered Tilly. 'There are monks all over the place. They're all dressed alike, in brown robes with hoods. Look! That one is carrying loaves of bread on a wooden spade to a big outdoor oven. And that one, right over there, beyond the fence, is chasing some runaway sheep,' she laughed.

'I bet the monk in the doorway of the nearest hut is in charge', mused Josh. 'He has a cross like this one round his neck.' This man suddenly turned and called to a young monk who was hoeing the garden.

'Cuthbert! See yon traveller nearing th' gate? Get thysen out there sharpish and greet 'im.'

'Do you think this is where Cuthbert came as a young man, long before he was a Saint?' suggested Tilly. They had moved a little closer, but the chain of the Cross they were holding got tangled in the thorn bush they were hiding behind and it was ripped out of their hands.

And back they were, in their hidey hole in the Cathedral floor, just as they had started.

'Josh! Tilly!'

'Mum's calling' Josh said, 'We're OK, Mum, we're just over here', he called back. 'We know our way around. We'll come and find you in the shop after a bit.'

And now for the facts ...

Holy Monks in a Huff!
(650 – 660)

Go Build a Monastery!

In the early days of Christianity in Northumbria, Alcfrith, the ruler of this part of Yorkshire, gave the land of about 30 farms for a monastery in Ripon. So, in about the year 650, the Prior

DM

of Melrose Abbey in Scotland sent Eata with a group of monks, including young Cuthbert, to build a monastery.

The Old Stone Crosses

A **Celtic** cross in the grounds of Ripon Cathedral Primary School roughly marks a spot where the wooden buildings of the Monastery might have stood. Only some bits of stone crosses and an old graveyard are left. Here the Celtic monks lived a simple life, farming the land and following the same religious rules as Melrose Abbey. They shaved their heads and wore rough homespun *habits.*

Young Cuthbert Meets an Angel

Cuthbert was the **Guestmaster** of the Monastery. His job was to welcome and care for travelling strangers. The **Venerable Bede's** writings tell us the following legend:

'Early one freezing winter's morning, Cuthbert found a visitor in the guest cell. He made the stranger welcome, brought him water and washed his weary feet. Then he left him to rest. He returned later to tell him that fresh bread would soon be ready for breakfast. But he discovered that the visitor had already left and strangely there were no footprints in the fresh snow. There was the smell of newly baked bread. Three new loaves sat on the doorstep. They were lily white, smelled of roses and tasted of honey. They could not be from the Monastery, where rough brown bread was eaten, so Cuthbert realised that the bread was heavenly bread and that his guest had been an angel.'

Cuthbert met many angels who helped him during his life.

Feud Between Two Sorts of Monks

Soon Wilfrid was made Bishop of York and Abbot of Ripon. He liked the Roman way of Christianity, which was practised in Rome and in other countries in Europe. The monks at Ripon did not want to change their way of worshipping God, which we call Celtic now, so they went back to Melrose in a huff.

Ripon Turns Roman

Wilfrid built his stone Church nearby and Ripon Monastery became **Benedictine.** Although the buildings were destroyed during the Saxon,

Viking and Norman periods, the Monastery lasted until the 11th Century when the Domesday Book shows a group of monks still at *'Ripun'*.

So What Became Of Cuthbert?

Cuthbert became Prior of Melrose and later Bishop of Lindisfarne, Holy Island. There he lived a simple life of prayer, very close to nature. He loved the sea birds, especially the eider ducks, which are still called '*Cuddy's* ducks'. After Cuthbert died, he was made a saint, and so his remains were precious. To keep his body safe from Vikings, it was moved around. In 995 it came to Ripon for a while. It was then taken to Durham, where it lies now.

UH

Above: Cuddy's ducks

Right: Monks carrying St Cuthbert's body

[Kath Hall]

9

Activities

Make Celtic Knot Patterns

Follow the pattern above with your finger and you will discover there is no beginning and no end !

Trace or scan the above pattern. Repeat it several times round the edge of a piece of paper. Colour it in. You have made a border for a page like the monks made in their manuscripts.

Make Coloured Trefoils

1. Trace the template on the left 3 times on coloured card
2. Fold each piece end to end
3. Cut the middle pieces out (cut on the dotted lines to remove the middle)
4. Open out the edge pieces
5. Stick the pieces onto a different coloured paper
6. Overlap the centre bits like the picture to make a trefoil
7. Stick the pieces onto a different coloured paper

Celtic Bread

The Celtic monks made round loaves, cutting a small cross in the top to help the bread rise. They used yeast and baked their risen dough in clay ovens outside their wooden buildings, because of the risk of fire.

Ordinary people did not always have yeast. Instead of loaves, they made flat unleavened bread, which could be baked on an iron griddle over an open fire.

Ask an adult to help you try this recipe, using a frying pan or griddle on a cooker.

Celtic Griddle Cakes

This recipe make 6 small cakes. You will need:

125g wholemeal flour
a pinch of salt
50g lard (or butter)
2 or 3 tablespoons milk

Put the flour and salt into a bowl. Rub the lard or butter in with your fingers until it is like fine breadcrumbs. Add just enough milk to make a firm dough.

Pinch off pieces of dough, shape into balls (about 4 cm) and flatten into cakes. Heat your greased griddle or pan. Cook cakes until lightly browned on both sides.

To make Sweet Griddle Cakes, add a little honey with the milk to the dough.

[Kath Hall]

Chapter 2

The Ripon Jewel

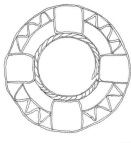

DT

Josh grasped the chest lid and began to lift – *crrreeeeaaak.*

'Quiet, someone will hear,' hissed his sister.

'No they won't, there's no-one here, and anyway, I told you to bring some oil for the hinges!'

When the lid was fully open, Tilly stretched out her hand. 'My turn this time,' she said, reaching into the chest. Her hand closed on a hard, round object that fitted neatly into the palm of her hand. In the flickering candlelight the twins looked down at sparkling jewels set in gold.

'Oh, a brooch,' breathed Tilly, 'but there's no pin!'

Around them the air grew thick and hazy, and suddenly they found themselves huddled in the corner of the dimly-lit crypt. In the wall niches Tilly could see ornate, bejewelled boxes, each with a glass side. Then they heard the sound of heavy footsteps descending steep stone stairs.

Two men came into view. The first looked to Josh like a monk of some kind, for he wore the black habit of a monk, and a heavy gold cross, hanging from a chain around his neck, glinted in the lamp-light. The other was most definitely a king, for he wore a golden crown on his head. His bright yellow tunic over dark blue leggings was topped by a rich red cloak fastened at his shoulder with a gold pin.

'So these are your relic caskets?' asked the king.

'Indeed Sire,' replied the monk, 'and this is our most precious relic', he said pointing to the largest casket. Tilly almost screamed – *the box contained a severed hand!*

'This is the hand of Saint Julius brought from Rome by our beloved Wilfrid, and he has adorned the casket with a jewel he especially loves.' Tilly wanted to be sick; the hand, which had been sliced off at the wrist, was mounted on an iron spike inside the casket, the palm facing outwards. The dark, decaying skin was stretched tightly over gnarled, bent fingers, the nails thick and yellow. It seemed to be reaching - grasping.

Tilly's head began to spin and she felt as though the floor would swallow her up. But eventually the haze cleared. The monk and the king were gone.

'Wow, wasn't that fantastic,' yelled Josh. 'Did you see that hand? Wait till I tell Dad, and it had that jewel on the casket as well. I wonder how old it is? Hundreds and hundreds of years I expect. We'd better put it back quick before someone comes.'

'And I want to go home,' said Tilly.

I wonder what happened to that hand, Josh thought to himself as they headed home; maybe I'll come and look for it another day.

DM

And now for the facts ...

Our Beloved Wilfrid – Who?

ilfrid was a very important person in our history. He was an Anglo-Saxon, born in the kingdom of Northumbria in 634. He was a friend to Kings and Queens, went to school in a monastery, travelled widely throughout England and France, and visited the Pope in Rome several times. He amassed great wealth that he used to build churches in which he placed the relics he brought from Rome. He had his wealth taken from him, was put in prison and was exiled from his beloved Northumbria for a time, but always he triumphed, and when he died in 710 he had changed our country forever.

How could one man change a country?

Well, he did a very simple thing – he set out the rules for Christian worship here in Britain - but to accomplish it took most of his life and this is how it happened:

Britain had once been ruled by the Romans, many of whom were Christians. Then, in the early 400's the Romans left and people from across the North Sea came. These people - the Anglo-Saxons - were 'Pagans'; that is people who knew nothing of Jesus and his teachings, and worshiped nature as they saw it all around them – life, death and re-birth in the changing seasons.

But Christianity didn't disappear completely from our island. It survived in the far North, the West and in Wales. Then in 596, as the Venerable Bede writes, Pope Gregory in Rome 'was inspired by God to send his servant Augustine with several other God-fearing monks to preach the word of God to the English nation.' And that was where it all began.

It wasn't long before Christian worship in our land was in a bit of a mess. You see, two very different 'churches' developed – the 'Celtic' and the 'Roman'. The Celtic tradition was brought to the North of England by Irish and Scottish monks whereas the Roman way of worship came to England with Augustine and missionaries from Rome. The first was 'pure and simple', the other 'colourful and ornate'. But the real problem was the dating of Easter.

The Match of the Century

In the spring of 664 Oswy, King of Northumbria (and a supporter of the Celtic tradition) was celebrating Easter Sunday, traditionally held with a special feast. At the same time his wife, Queen Eanfleda (a supporter of the Roman tradition), was still observing Lent, a time of fasting. As you can imagine, the court was in turmoil. The king had had enough and decided it was time to settle things, once and for all. He asked his friend Hilda, the abbess of a monastery at Whitby, to host a meeting of churchmen who would, with himself, settle the date of Easter for everyone. This meeting became known as the Synod of Whitby.

The Celtic churchmen were captained by Bishop Colman and the Roman churchmen by Bishop Agilbert. Bishop Colman spoke first saying he followed the customs laid down by his forefathers, men who loved God; and that these customs owed their origin to the teaching of the blessed evangelist, Saint John himself, the disciple especially loved by Jesus.

(And it's a goal to the Celts)

It was Bishop Agilbert's turn next. He asked the King to allow Wilfrid to speak in his place and so it was that Wilfrid began the task that would take him the rest of his life to complete. He was most eloquent, explaining how the Roman way of reckoning Easter was now followed by all men across the world and that the only people who stupidly disagreed were these few Celts.

(And the Romans equalize)

HE And then he told the King not to forget that the founder of these customs was the Blessed Saint Peter, to whom Jesus had given the keys to Heaven, and who had lived and died in Rome. (And follow up with a brilliant winning goal).

HE

(Final score: Celts 1, Romans 2)

Another problem was the way monks cut their hair, (called the tonsure). The tonsure was an outward sign that these men had dedicated their lives to Christ. The monks following the Celtic tradition grew their hair much longer and shaved off the front above the forehead. The Roman tonsure kept the hair short and a circle was shaved at the top of the head.

Of course King Oswy ruled in favour of Bishop Agilbert and the Roman way, but Wilfrid had made many enemies that day. You might imagine a Synod as a game, but it was very serious indeed and the decisions taken were important, not only for Wilfrid's remaining life, but also in helping to shape our history.

Fire, fire, burning bright

Details from the Cathedral's 'St Wilfrid' window – here the 'fire' that heralded the saint's birth and, below, Wilfrid

But how had Wilfrid come to be included in such an important meeting? Well, Wilfrid's father was a Thegn – that's a nobleman, who served the king. He was head of the village, lived in the biggest house and was very rich. The day Wilfrid was born people thought they saw flames in the house and ran to get water; but then they found the house wasn't burning after all – it was a sign that Wilfrid was very special.

Enter the wicked step-mother

Wilfrid was a very happy boy and, with a rich family, he had the best of everything. But then his world changed. His mother died and his father got a new wife. Wilfrid and his step-mother didn't get on together at all, so Wilfrid was sent away – to the royal court. Now Wilfrid not only had the best of everything, but there were lots of important people to meet. It was very exciting.

Oh no, not school!

Soon Queen Eanfleda said Wilfrid had to go to school, and she sent him to the monastery on the island of Lindisfarne. The monks taught Wilfrid to read and write but the monastery was Celtic, and that meant 'pure and simple' – food, dress, religious services – the whole way of life. In fact, for Wilfrid it was very harsh after the life he had

17

been used to; he even had to work as a servant, fetching and carrying for the older monks. Lindisfarne was also very isolated for a young boy and Wilfrid hated everything about it except for his studies.

Wilfrid's 'Gap Year'

When his schooling was over Wilfrid decided to go to Rome. Queen Eanfleda agreed to support him and he was soon on his way. Travel then was very difficult and dangerous, but he made many friends who helped him on his journey. In France, he stayed with the Bishop of Lyon who wanted to give him lots of money, and a wife, but Wilfrid said 'no thank you' and continued on his journey.

HE

Money and a wife for Wilfrid? 'No, thanks'

Making important friends

Wilfrid liked the grand stone buildings in Rome, (the Saxons only used wood). He met the Pope and studied with Archdeacon Boniface, a wise and learned man. Here religious life was the 'colourful and ornate' kind – churches adorned with beautiful statues and painted walls; priests who wore exquisite robes and chanted to the sound of wonderful music; the smell of exotic incense. It was so different from Lindisfarne!

Wilfrid wanted the people at home to worship like this and he wanted to be part of it also. He studied hard and that is why, when he returned

---

? ? ? Did You Know ? ? ?

The Ripon Jewel, made of gold and semi-precious gems, was found near the Cathedral in 1976. It might have been used as an ornament for one of Wilfrid's relic caskets or a holy book.

home, Bishop Agilbert asked him to speak at the Synod of Whitby.

How to get a monastery...

While Wilfrid was in Rome, his friend Alcfrith, the son of King Oswy, had given land in Ripon to Eata, Abbot of Melrose, to start a new monastery. He had hoped the monastery would follow the Roman way but Eata preferred the Celtic way and wouldn't change. So, when Wilfrid came home asking for land to build a monastery, Alcfrith gave Eata an ultimatum – change or leave. Eata left (taking many of the monks with him) and Wilfrid became Abbot.

...and make it special

The monastery buildings, being Saxon, were wooden. Wilfrid couldn't change that right away but he could build a new church. Soon craftsmen from France and Italy, skilled in the use of stone, were hard at work. The

DM

church, dedicated to Saint Peter, sitting on high ground for all to see, was a wonder.

A man called Stephen who knew and loved Wilfrid wrote his life story. In his book he says, 'in Ripon he built and completed from the foundations in the earth up to the roof, a church of dressed stone, supported by various columns and side aisles.' Of the altar, he says Wilfrid, 'vested it in purple woven with gold.' Finally, he says Wilfrid provided among other treasures a marvel of beauty never before heard of '...the four gospels to be written out in letters of gold on purpled parchment and illuminated. He also ordered jewellers to construct for the books a case all made of purest gold and set with most precious gems.'

Wilfrid certainly wanted his church here in Ripon to be very special; he

DM

even brought a singing–master from Kent to teach the monks how to chant properly. Can you imagine what it must have been like, filled with rich colours, treasures and the relics he brought from Rome? Wilfrid would have kept his most important treasures and relics in the Crypt – the only part of his church to survive. You can still visit it today below the crossing at the centre of our fine Cathedral.

Rich man...

Wilfrid loved the grandeur of the Roman church and spent the rest of his life building monasteries and churches where people could worship in this way. He grew very rich and powerful and became a bishop. Kings were afraid of his power and tried to stop him, but Wilfrid went to Rome each time and spoke to the Pope, who always sided with him.

DM

One Saxon ruler, King Egfrith, who was jealous of Wilfrid's wealth and influence, said that Wilfrid had bribed the Pope. He put Wilfrid in prison and took away all his money and land. Wilfrid was only let out when he promised to leave Northumbria.

...Poor man

Wilfrid travelled widely, preaching and helping people. Once he came upon people who were starving because their crops had failed. Wilfrid taught them how to fish and thereby saved their lives. Soon they, too, were Christians.

Sometimes it was said he even performed miracles, like the time he saw a poor mother carrying her dead baby, which he brought back to life.

Death!

When he was seventy-one Wilfrid had a dream. The Archangel Michael told him that he would only live four more years. He decided to give away all his money and treasure. Some he gave to the poor; some he sent to the church in Rome; some he left to his monasteries in Ripon and Hexham; the rest he gave to his friends.

He was in a place called Oundle when he died but he had left instructions that his body was to be buried in his favourite place – Ripon.

? ? ? **Did You Know** ? ? ?

Relics are the remains of saints or objects associated with them such a bone, hair, teeth, cloth or even blood. They were said to have miraculous powers of healing and were an important part of worship in the early days of the Christian Church. Wilfrid brought many relics back from his travels. The Roman Catholic Church placed relics under the altar stones of all their churches. Protestants do not venerate relics.

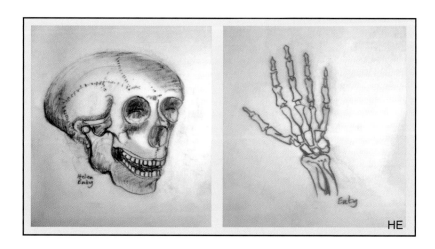

[Lynne Ditchburn]

Activities

Time for Tea and Cake

Did you know that monks kept bees so they could make candles from the honeycomb wax? They used the honey like sugar (which they didn't know about then). In the autumn they would dry fruit to use during the long winters. Here is a recipe for you to make little cakes just as they did. You may need a grown-up to help.

John Ditchburn

First measure out your ingredients –
125grams of porridge oats
60grams of unsalted butter
25grams of dried fruits like apricots or apples
2 large tablespoons of runny honey
½ level teaspoon of ground cinnamon

Now to begin –
Turn the oven on to 375F/180C
You need to melt the butter gently in a saucepan –don't let it burn – and when it's melted turn off the heat.
Now you can add all the other ingredients, mixing them together really well.
Next you need a well greased baking sheet (pour a little oil onto the sheet and spread it all around).
Drop spoonfuls of the mixture onto the greased baking sheet and then use the back of the spoon to flatten each one a little.
Now, into the hot oven with them until they turn a golden colour – about 10 minutes or a little longer.
When they are done take the cakes out of the oven and gently lift them onto a wire baking rack to cool down.
Finally pour a glass of apple juice to drink while you eat your delicious **Honey, Oat and Spiced Cakes** – Yummy!!!

[Lynne Ditchburn]

23

Another Busy Day
in Saxon Ripon

A story by pupils at Holy Trinity C of E Junior School, Year 3

My family and I had arrived in Ripon in 640 AD after a long sea voyage in a large shallow-bottomed boat from our homeland across the North Sea. We, along with many other families came over the water for the

promise of better farm land left by the Romans.

Families before us had settled and gradually moved further and further inland following the rivers. That's how we ended up in Ripon. I must say, my family and I are much happier here.

I'd like to tell you about a typical day in my life here in Saxon Ripon. My name is Hilda and I'm 8 years old, that's what Mother tells me. I live

with my Mother, Father and my older brother. He's called Edgar. We're good friends really but he does annoy me sometimes especially when I'm trying to help Mother with the chores.

Today I woke up to the sound of cockerels crowing and noisy

villagers clattering about in the workshop. I sat up and rubbed my eyes. Why does everyone set out to the workshop so early in the morning? It was far too noisy for me to sleep much longer. I had slept well though because the logs in the firebox had burned nearly all night and kept us all warm. I hauled myself up off my straw bed and got out my long white dress and head cloth. My leather shoes and belt were hung up outside the door. I got ready quickly because there was a lot of work to be done. I remembered to put on my favourite belt buckle that I got for my birthday. Mother and Father bought it from a travelling trader who passed by our village.

I tidied my blankets and went to help Mother with the daily chores. I started by breaking our fast with a small piece of bread, baked by my Mother and me the day before, and a drink. Father and Edgar were already at work on the land. They would be back for something to eat

later. Meanwhile, Mother and I started to make soup for the evening's meal in the hall. We put all the ingredients into a big cooking pot and then we poured water over the vegetables. It would be boiling over the fire all day.

The land is good and we grow lots of interesting crops. All the villagers farm the nearby land together. Edgar and Father work there every day. There's always plenty to keep them very busy. Over to Edgar who has lots to tell us about man's work….

Our days are always busy, busy, busy. We spend our time hunting, fishing, farming the land and working in the craft house. We leave the spinning and the weaving of cloth, the sewing and the cooking to the ladies and the girls. We children have learnt what to do by watching and helping our parents. It's very hard work and I feel very tired by the end of the day. Every morning is an early start. This morning I was up feeding the chickens whilst Father was busy in the fields. Mother and Hilda were still fast asleep. We would come back later for something to eat when they were awake.

I started by collecting the eggs which can be anywhere and then went to sort out the pigs.

They are my favourite. I love them so much. They are also important animals because they have big litters. This means we always have lots of meat to eat. The sheep and goats, which give us milk and wool as well as meat, graze on our land too. Each year some of our fields are left unused or 'fallow' and they graze there. The manure from the animals helps to make the fields more fertile

for growing spelt, wheat and barley, the following year.

We have just got some cattle into Ripon. Father said these will not only give us milk to drink and meat to eat but also their hides will be made into leather. We will be able to turn this leather into shoes and belts so these will be very useful.

After a break and something to eat, Father and I got back to work. Because it is spring time, we spent the rest of the day digging ditches and sowing seeds, beans, flax and herbs. On summer days we spread manure, mend fences, make fish traps, shear sheep and cut firewood. In autumn we reap, we beat the flax, kill animals to eat in winter and cut hay for animal feed. When winter comes we spend our days ploughing, threshing, cutting wood, pruning the orchards and doing indoor jobs.

By the end of our working day we had got a lot of jobs done. Father and I were very tired, very hungry and very dirty. I couldn't wait for something to eat and drink. Father was pleased with me today because I had worked very hard. I'm getting better at all the different jobs but I'm glad when our work is finished. When we get back home we will be just in time for our evening meal in the hall. I can't wait!

That's all from Edgar. Thank you Edgar. Now back to my day.

While the soup was cooking, we had lots of other jobs to be getting on with. My first job was to spin the flax in to linen for our clothes.

Meanwhile, my best friend Annis was collecting sheep's wool to spin into yarn. Me and Annis sat by the bright light of the burning candle. Annis was making leggings for the boys, whilst I was making a beautiful new

head cloth as a present for Mother. Weaving is quite hard but I think I quite get the hang of it now. Sometimes it does become a bit tricky (lucky Mother is usually there to help me out). By the end of the day we had a new pair of leggings dyed brown with onion skins and a beautiful white head cloth with red and blue wavy

lines across it.

Before long, Father and Edgar were home, so then we could go to the hall to meet our family and friends for something to eat. Everyone was rushing into the hall. It was very noisy! When we sat down, the yummy smell of freshly baked bread drifted up my nostrils. It smelled delicious. Vegetable and barley soup too. My favourite! I had two helpings and stopped there.

We had to clear away very quickly because we had a storyteller in tonight. I was very excited! We were going to be told the story about Beowulf, a hero who killed the terrible monster Grendel. It was quite scary but I enjoyed it very much!

When we got back to the house, Mother had some very important jobs to get on with and wanted me out of the way. So I went off to my bed to play with my wooden toy animals for a bit before I fell asleep.

Another busy day has flown by. I wonder if it'll be just the same again tomorrow!

[Holy Trinity CE Junior School, Year 3]

Recipe for Vegetable and Barley Soup – Saxon style
1 leek – peeled and sliced
1 onion – peeled and sliced
200g peas
Handful of chopped cabbage
200g (pearl) barley
1 bay leaf
Pinch of sage
Pinch of salt

Put all the ingredients into a pan. Just cover with water and bring to the boil.
Turn the heat down and simmer for 40 minutes or until the barley is soft.
Take out the bay leaf.
Ladle into a bowl and eat with a big piece of bread.

Chapter 3

The Longship Brooch

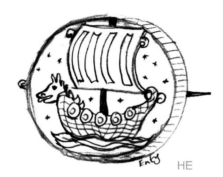
HE

Reaching deep into the chest, Josh felt a tiny, cold object and slowly pulled out a beautiful silver brooch that looked to him like a long pointed ship. At one end of the long ship was a dragon's head, and along its side were rows of oars and round shields.

'I've seen pictures of boats like this before', said Tilly.

'Who do you think it belonged to?' asked Josh. Suddenly they became aware of the smell of smoke and the sound of screams filling their ears. In front of them, they saw the high walls of a church cracking as dust and smoke filled the air.

'What is happening to the Cathedral?' shouted Tilly. They saw monks dressed in long black robes and the monks were pleading with groups of soldiers to leave in peace. The soldiers wore rough red tunics, their heads covered by metal and chain mail helmets. Groups of soldiers were attacking the Cathedral with huge battering rams, throwing burning torches, and smashing the beautiful windows with metal axes. 'What are you doing?' yelled Tilly.

'Be quiet, Tilly, you will get us killed!' whispered Josh, putting his hand over his sister's mouth and pulling her out of sight.

The twins quickly ran behind a huge yew tree in the dip behind the church. The pair gasped as the white walls began to tumble down in front of them. They could see flames licking at stone arches, curved wooden beams and the beautiful carvings inside what was left of the building. Shaven headed monks were running away from the flames, their arms full with golden statues and bright jewel-covered books. Other monks were kneeling in front of the building praying loudly.

'What is going on here?' murmured Josh. Nearby, the twins could see children dressed in colourful robes. Their robes were fastened with decorated brooches and pins and the children had golden and red hair woven into plaits and elaborate braids. The twins realised that they had only seen clothing like this in history books of times long, long ago. Tilly held the silver brooch tighter in her hand as some of the children tried to pull their parents away to safety.

The twins dipped further behind the tree as the walls continued to topple. The soldiers smashed and set fire to everything inside the crumbling building.

'What have these poor people done to deserve this?' Tilly murmured to herself.

A soldier was shouting as a group of men tried to pull him away and he struck at them with his sword: 'We carry out the King's orders. We Saxons will teach you not to harbour those Viking scum! How could you live in peace with those people and make them your own? No trace of your precious St Wilfrid and his church will remain. That will teach you and the Norsemen a lesson!'

As the smoke began to clear, all went quiet. Tilly began to creep out from behind the tree.

'Wait! It could still be dangerous!' pleaded Josh as he crawled out to follow her. They gasped at what lay before them. The beautiful building was now just a huge pile of smoking rubble with all its glorious decorations smashed, burnt, or stripped away. A stone cross lay broken in front of the ruin and all around were the bodies of monks and others who had not escaped the soldiers' weapons.

'Look' shouted Josh as they got nearer. 'See, there! There's an entrance going underground!'

Tilly noticed a very small, old passageway that went down into the stone floor. It was below the spot where the middle of the church had stood.

'And there's another hole in the ground, a bit further on,' said Josh. 'Is it a tunnel into something below the Cathedral?'

'Perhaps there is a precious part of the building that those Saxon warriors couldn't destroy', whispered Tilly.

Just as she spoke, everything changed again. The air was suddenly clearer and it was very quiet. The twins realised they were back in the Cathedral in front of the mysterious chest. Tilly was still holding the silver brooch tightly in her hand.

'Let me see that' said Josh 'I know where I've seen that ship before, the sort with the dragon's head. Those long ships were the ones used by the Vikings. And imagine, we thought the Vikings were the ones who wrecked the churches!'

DM

And now for the facts ...

The Vikings

The Warning!

 or many years, the Anglo Saxons had lived in peace in Ripon. St Wilfrid's stone church, which had been built in 672, was at the heart of the town. Ripon had strong links with other important places in the north like Lindisfarne, York and Whitby. In the year AD 793, everything was to change! The Anglo Saxon Chronicle, (the book that recorded the history of that time), says that there were signs that something awful was going to happen:

"This year came dreadful fore-warnings over the land of the Northumbrians, terrifying the people most woefully: these were immense sheets of light rushing through the air, and whirlwinds, and fiery dragons flying across the firmament. These tremendous tokens were soon followed by a great famine: and not long after… the harrowing inroads of heathen men made lamentable havoc in the church of God in Holy-Island."

What was going to happen?

The Vikings are coming!

These fearsome "heathen men" were the Vikings. They sailed across the North Sea from the lands we now call Norway, Denmark, and Sweden and landed at Lindisfarne (Holy Island). They came in long curved wooden boats, called longships. These were often decorated with

AG

AG

dragon heads or carvings of fierce animals
on the curved end of the boat.

Run away!

It must have been a terrifying sight as the
Vikings landed and ran out of the boats
towards the island. They attacked the wealthy
monastery and abbey, killed many monks, and took precious statues,
gold, jewels, and people to sell as slaves. The Saxons were horrified that
anyone could attack their holy place but this was only the first of many
attacks on churches, monasteries, and villages. The English soon became
terrified of the Vikings!

The Vikings reach Ripon!

After this the Vikings, also known as Danes or Norsemen, kept returning
to England. The first Vikings came to raid and steal (the name "Viking"
comes from their language, Norse, and means "pirate" or "raider") and this
is how we usually think of them. But most Vikings who came to England
later were peaceful, wanting to sell goods that they collected from many
countries, or to farm here. Vikings needed places to farm as the land in
their own countries was poor. They soon began to take over land in places
like Ripon, which they could reach by sailing along the rivers in their low-
bottomed boats.

Vikings were excellent sailors who travelled thousands of miles in their
longboats. They sailed all the way to the south of Italy, and up the rivers
into Russia and even reached North America! The Norsemen were also
wonderful craftsmen. They made beautiful jewellery in gold and silver.
They also carved stones and wood and were excellent graffiti artists who
left carvings on stones wherever they went!

The Vikings did not write their stories down but loved tales and poetry, especially about gods and heroes. These tales were passed down by retelling them for hundreds of years, and most towns would have had a skald, a story teller.

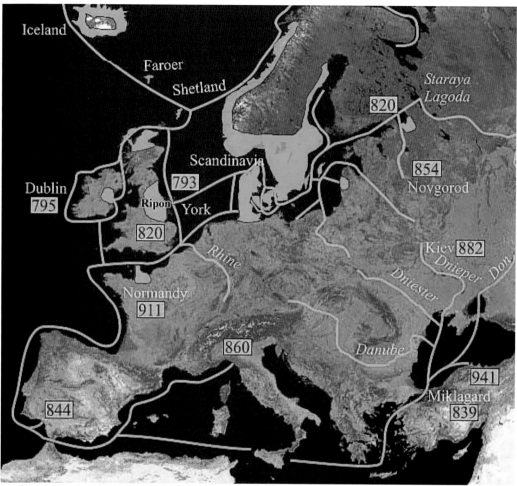

Light green areas are main Viking settlements and the blue lines show some of the journeys they made

? ? ?   Did You Know   ? ? ?

The Vikings had their own alphabet called "Runes", which looked like marks. They did not have enough runes for every sound, so spelling must have been very difficult!

Thor and his mighty hammer!

The Vikings worshipped their gods at home or in special outdoor places. They had many gods: Odin, who was the most powerful, Loki, the god of mischief, and the goddesses Frey and Freya. Their favourite god was Thor, who carried a great stone hammer, called Mjollnir, which had magic powers. Thor was the god of war, thunder and lightning and many Vikings wore tiny hammer-shaped charms around their necks for good luck. They also believed in giants and dwarfs who made trouble.

A good-luck charm worn around the neck

The Dragon Slayer and the Cross

Gradually, the Vikings began to understand Christianity and, in AD 878, the Viking King, Guthrum, was baptised as a Christian. From then on many more Danes converted (changed to Christian ways), but often the Viking and Christian beliefs were mixed together. In 1970, part of a stone cross from the time of the Vikings was found near Ripon Cathedral. The crosspiece is carved with the figure of Sigurd who was a hero in one of the Norse tales. In the story, Sigurd kills the dragon Fafnir. He then burns his thumb when he roasts the dragon's heart, and the Ripon carving shows him sucking his thumb! Although the cross is the sign of Jesus, we can see that the carver wasn't quite ready to give up the old Norse ways or his hero, Sigurd!

The Sigurd stone fragment, showing the Norse dragon-slayer sucking his thumb

The Masham Skeletons

In Masham, fifty-seven skeletons dating from AD 679 to AD 1011 were discovered in an old graveyard that had been covered for hundreds of years. The skeletons were buried in the Christian way, facing east. The bones were tested and scientists found that the later bodies were of people with both Saxon and Viking DNA. This means that the two groups lived together peacefully and possibly inter-married. The burials did not have any grave goods which shows that they worshipped as Christians. We think that the same was taking place in Ripon and, at that time, people with Viking and Saxon ancestors could have been worshipping at St Wilfrid's Church. The Masham Bones were reburied in 2009 in a ceremony which used Norse and Anglo Saxon language and you can see their new gravestone in Masham churchyard.

Some of the remains of people of mixed Saxon and Viking heritage found in an excavated burial site in Masham. They were reburied in the nearby churchyard 2009

Photo courtesy of Kevin Cale Community Archaeology

Photo courtesy of Mrs E. Witton, Pott and Agill Study Group

Give us more gold!

In around AD 865, thousands more Vikings began to arrive in what we call "The Great Viking Army". In 886 the first English King, Alfred the Great,

agreed with the Viking King Guthrum to divide England into two areas to keep the peace. Ripon was in the north part under Viking rule or "Danelaw" and the Saxons kept the south west. The Saxons later had to pay gold and silver to the Danes to stop them attacking. This was called "Danegeld" (Danish gold). However, the Vikings kept asking for more and more gold to stop them taking land. Soon the Saxons were fighting the Vikings again and this would bring disaster to Ripon!

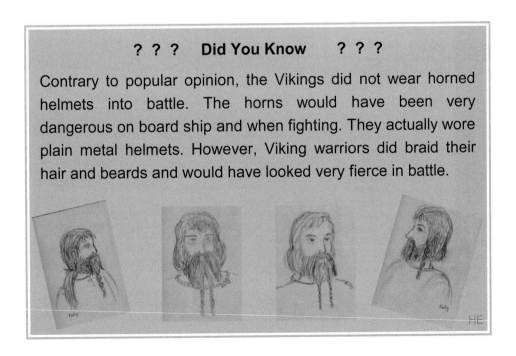

? ? ?   Did You Know   ? ? ?

Contrary to popular opinion, the Vikings did not wear horned helmets into battle. The horns would have been very dangerous on board ship and when fighting. They actually wore plain metal helmets. However, Viking warriors did braid their hair and beards and would have looked very fierce in battle.

Refuge in Ripon!

In 926, the Saxon King Athelstan, (the grandson of King Alfred), visited Ripon after winning battles in the North. To celebrate his victory, he granted Ripon "Liberty". Having "liberty"

meant that Ripon had its own laws. In addition, anyone who wanted to take shelter from an enemy or after committing a crime, could ask to be protected (or given sanctuary) here. If you were granted sanctuary you would have to live under the protection of the Minster and its laws. The area in which "liberty" applied was within a mile of Ripon Minster. This area was marked by eight sanctuary crosses. The only one left now is just the bottom part, at Sharow. The Sanctuary Way walk around Ripon follows close to part of the mile boundary.

? ? ?　Did You Know　? ? ?

The Vikings believed that if they were killed in battle or were heroes, they would go to a glorious place called Valhalla when they died.

They also thought that ordinary people would go to a boring place called Niflheim!

The Cathedral Burns!

In the 940s, the Viking King, Eric Bloodaxe, took over York and Ripon. Although Norse and Saxons were living together in peace here, the Saxon

DM

King, Eadred, wanted to push the Vikings out of the North forever. So he got a large army together to attack the Viking lands, including York and Ripon.

In around AD 948 Saxon King Eadred's army attacked Ripon, set fire to the monastery, and burnt St Wilfrid's beautiful church to the ground. A large area around the minster was also destroyed and we think that many people were killed. This must have been a terrible time for the monks and people living here and the Saxon writer Eadmer wrote that the ruined church at Ripon became the home "not of priests but of wild beasts".

What happened next?

Although Eric Bloodaxe was beaten, the Vikings continued to attack England and, within one hundred years, the Danish King Canute ruled the whole country. In 1066 the Normans, (who were descended from the

Vikings in Northern France), conquered England and soon began to build a huge minster at Ripon where St Wilfrid's church had stood.

The two faces of a silver coin dating from the rule of Eric Bloodaxe. One side shows a sword, the other a Christian cross.

? ? ?   **Did You Know**   ? ? ?

That Vikings did not go to school? Their parents taught boys how to farm, build and fight. The girls were taught how to weave, cook and look after the farm if the men went to war.

[Carol Priestley]

Activities

Do YOU live on a Viking street?

We do not know exactly when the Vikings reached Ripon, but think that they lived around here on and off for nearly 200 years. We know that they were here because Ripon, like York, has many streets with Viking words in their name. Most of the streets around the Cathedral have names ending in "gate". This was the Norse word for street or way and Kirkgate means "Church Street". The words "skell", "garth", "dale", "thwaite", "gill" and "by" all come from the Viking language. How many Viking street names you can see on the map of Ripon on the next page?

Can YOU read Anglo-Saxon?

These two sentences from the Anglo-Saxon Chronicle describe what happened in Ripon:

"Her Eadred cyning oferhergode eall Norohymbra land for paem pe hi haefdon genumen him Yryc to cyninge. Ond pa on paere hergunge waes maere mynster forbaernd aet Rypon, paet Sanctus Wilfred getimbrede. "

If you got stuck, here is the English translation:

"Here King Eadred raided across all the land of Northumbria, because they had taken Eric (Bloodaxe, son of Harald Fine-hair) for their king … … ... and on the raid then the famous minster at Ripon, which St Wilfrid built, was burned."

[Carol Priestley]

43

Central Ripon Streetmap

(See Activities section on previous page)

Once Upon a Viking Day

A story by pupils at Ripon Cathedral Primary School, Year 3

My family travelled from Norway by boat to Britain in 870. We used

to live in York but we have just moved to Ripon. My father is called Ulf. His name was picked by his father. This is a tradition. Ulf means wolf. My mother is called Orm, which means snake and I am called Thorwald after the God Thor. I have a younger sister called Bjorn. We don't have last names.

The rest of my family are still in Norway and will come over to live with us when we have found a new settlement and built our houses big enough for us all to live in. Our house is called a longhouse. It is made from wood and our sloping roof is thatched with reeds. We all live and sleep in one big room. In winter we will all sleep around the fire to keep warm and wrap up in animal fur and woven blankets. Sometimes in winter our animals share our house. It can be a bit smelly but the animals help to keep us warm.

The walls of our longhouse are thick so if people came to attack us we would be safe. In the middle of the room we have a big fire which keeps us warm. The fire is lit all day and all night. Mother and Bjorn cook all the meals over the fire. It is really smoky in our

house. We have benches to sit at to eat our food and we sleep on them. We have some other buildings that we use as workshops and storehouses. When I was 10 years old I could help father make tools and weapons in the workshop. This is his trade. I have made combs, brooches and helped father make tools from fish and animal bones.

Today I woke up really early. I could smell the porridge mother was cooking for us on the fire for our breakfast. Mother always tells us to eat all our breakfast because we only have 2 meals a day. Me and Bjorn don't go to school. We can't read and write. Mother and father don't have enough money to send us so we have to work around the settlement. I look after the animals and learn to fight and fetch wood. Bjorn learns about how to run a household properly from mother. It's getting colder so mother and Bjorn have been weaving wool and thread to make some new warmer clothes. We have to make all our clothes.

We have sheep, goats and cattle. I have to go and feed the animals but because it is so cold I don't want to go outside. I want to sit next to the fire and finish my porridge. I know I have to do my jobs because father has gone on his own hunting. I wonder what we will have for supper: a fox, a wild boar or wild birds? He will be out all day so I am in charge. We are also looking after our neighbour's goats, geese and chickens.

My father goes hunting for our food a lot. Yesterday father caught some fish from the nearby river. When he came back we could see that

he had caught some big ones. He gave them to mother and Bjorn who took the guts out and then cooked them and served them to us around the fire with some apple juice. Bjorn helped my mother pick the apples from the orchard near our house. She helped her clean them and squeeze them to make apple juice for us. It is really tasty. We also grow plums and berries in our orchard. We have a garden to grow onions, peas and cabbages. We grow oats, barley and wheat and grind them to make flour, porridge and ale.

Sometimes some of the food like meat and fish that me and father catch is smoked to stop them going bad and stored for the long snowy winters

so we don't starve. We keep all the food in our storehouse.

It is evening time and we are all sitting around the fire. We are having hare and vegetables for supper which mother has cooked in her big cauldron. I am really hungry. All I had to eat today was

porridge for breakfast and a few berries which I found near the river. It will soon be our bedtime, but father said we can play a board game and listen to some of mother's poems about the God Thor. Tomorrow Bjorn and mother are going to make winter clothes from the deer skin that father went hunting for yesterday and boots from the hare skin. I hope that the weather will be dry soon because we have to mend our longboat. It was damaged on the long journey from Norway. We will use the tools that I helped make from the fish bones.

After supper we always play games before we go to bed. I played with my toy boat, spinning top and wooden weapons. Bjorn has a model horse and dolls. We make our own music. We made musical instruments out of wood, bones and animal skins.

We will all go to bed at the same time after brushing our teeth. Me and Bjorn wrap ourselves in our woven blankets and sleep next to the fire. I hope Bjorn does not keep me up all night coughing like last night. Mother has made her some medicines from herbs to try and help. We have an early start tomorrow, father is going to sell the tools and weapons at the market. Sometimes father sells things for silver or barters for something else we might need. It might be animals for our farm or pots for mother. Last week father got me some new leather shoes.

Tomorrow night two people in our settlement are getting married and tomorrow night we will all have a feast. We will all join in and help cook food. We will eat and drink, read stories and play music on the instruments we have made. People from our settlement will be entertaining us by dressing as jesters and juggling.

Chapter 4

The Green Man

PH

'What on earth are we going to find next?' asked Josh, turning to his sister. 'Your turn to feel inside the chest, when I've oiled the hinges a bit to stop it creaking so loudly.'

Tilly pushed her hand inside the slit between the heavy lid and the side of the chest and groped around. She could feel some cold stone with interesting bumps on it. With a bit of twisting and turning she pulled it through the slit. 'It's a face. But it's not an ordinary person.'

'It's weird,' said Josh, putting his hand on it too. 'Look at the curly beard with pine cones and leaves in it, as if he is part of a tree.'

'Oh, I think I know what it is,' Tilly replied. 'He's a Green Man, leftover from a time when people worshipped Nature. There is a face just like this, high up above the shop in here, carved in the Middle Ages, when they believed in all sorts of strange creatures.'

Then *woosh,* they suddenly felt cold, despite the heavy woollen clothes they were now wearing. They could not see properly.

'It's a bit gloomy and smoky in here,' said Tilly. They had landed right in the Middle Ages, when the Minster windows were full of glowing coloured glass, making little patterns on the stone floor where the light filtered through. Candles, burning on several altars all around, lit up

49

coloured carvings and showed that the walls were brightly painted too. She spotted a few weary looking people kneeling quietly in front of one altar with an open gold casket, sparkling with red jewels. She narrowed her eyes to see more clearly.

'Oh my gosh, it's got a head in it!' she exclaimed.

Josh leant forward and could just make out some writing on the front - 'Wilfridus.' How gruesome; it must be the head of St Wilfrid. Why have people come to see that? And where's the rest of his body?'

'Watch out!' said Tilly, pulling her brother safely back, as two sweaty burly men came tramping rudely past them. They were rubbing dust off their hands, as one muttered to the another,

'Have we nearly done with carting them big blocks for t'wall at t'back? None of them marauding Scots will get past that.' These men were followed sharply by another man in a long garb, with a cord tied around his middle like a belt. He was hurrying to a corner tower to ring the bell which soon began to sound.

'There must be some sort of Service about to begin', said Tilly. 'I know they used to have a lot every day. Let's listen'

Very soon a whole procession of men, young and old, in all sorts of long flowing clothes, some fancy and some plain, shuffled into the building and disappeared through the archway towards the altar. A hand-bell sounded a note and the singers all began to chant together in a strange language.

Josh whispered, 'I can't understand that at all. It must be that dead language Latin. And who are they? They can't *all* be priests!' The chanting went on and on.

Suddenly Tilly said, 'I feel a bit sick; there's a new smell wafting through. Is it perfume of some sort?'

'I think it must be incense', said Josh. 'Did you see the ball on a chain which one of the priests was swinging? They burn incense in that. I think it's to make things pure. At least it covers up the sweaty smells of those scruffy men!'

'Ouch!' said Josh, 'You've dropped that stone on my foot'

And suddenly back they were, once again in their everyday clothes and in their own time, just as though nothing had happened.

50

And now for the facts ...

The Colourful, Smelly & Pious Middle Ages

ometime during the 11th Century, when the Monastery came to an end, monks were replaced with Canons. The Minster became very powerful, owning half of Ripon. It was the largest and most important building for many miles around. The best craftsmen worked to make it more and more beautiful. Not only a local church and a place of *pilgrimage*, it was also a town meeting place and a centre of learning, music and the arts. But times were dangerous and there was a constant threat of violence and disease.

Canons and priests galore and visiting monks

The Archbishop of York was a very important man in the Middle Ages, with a palace near Ripon Minster. Being a busy man, he did not visit the Minster very often, but one of his jobs was to inspect the Minster from time to time, to make sure that the priests were doing their jobs properly. On a daily basis, seven Canons and eighteen other priests worshipped in the Minster and also cared for people all around Ripon. The Canons wore their own splendid *vestments*, showing how important they were.

The priests were learned people, who could read and write. The Minster once owned many wonderful *manuscripts*, handwritten in Latin. The Brotherton Library in Leeds keeps safely some surviving precious manuscripts, including the 13th Century Ripon Bible which has beautifully coloured *illuminated letters*.

At Christmas in 1134, thirteen *Benedictine* Monks from St Mary's Abbey

York arrived at Ripon. Archbishop Thurstan had given them some land to found a new **Cistercian** Monastery with a very simple way of life. The day after Christmas they walked to the valley of the River Skell, where they built Fountains Abbey. So, the black Benedictine monks

PH

became the white Cistercian monks. Every year many people join the Boxing Day Walk between Ripon Cathedral and Fountains Abbey to remember the walk undertaken by the enterprising monks so long ago.

Live music absolutely every day

Eight times daily, from very early in the morning to very late at night, the Canons, priests and six male singers chanted the **Choral Offices** in Latin. They filled every single seat in the **Choir**. Before the end of the 14th Century there was no organ, so they sang unaccompanied **Plainsong**, taking their notes from a hand bell. The singers stood throughout the services, but old and sick singers could lean on the little ledges on tip-up seats called **misericords** or mercy seats. Rushes were strewn in the Choir in winter to keep the singers warm. Ordinary people were not allowed into the Choir.

Ding Dong Bell!

The Mary Bell announced the daily Mass of the Virgin Mary in the Lady Loft.

Another large bell, called the Klank Knoll, came from Fountains Abbey in the 14th Century. It tolled for the dead and was especially busy when the Black Death visited Ripon more than once. Over one third of the population died of the plague during this century.

Tourists flock to see Wilfrid's bones

Travelling **pilgrims** walked or came on horseback to visit Saint Wilfrid's **Shrine**, perhaps hoping for a cure or a blessing or doing penance for their sins. When Archbishop Grey needed money in the 13th century, to make the Minster bigger, he granted indulgences to pilgrims in exchange for money towards the building works. He decided to rebury Wilfrid's bones in three parts, all around the Minster. Some historians believe that the zig zag stones in the Chapel of Justice and Peace came from Wilfrid's tomb which was probably

---

? ? ?   Did You Know   ? ? ?

Medieval pilgrims wore badges to show that they were on their way home from a shrine. Many badges had the picture of a saint on them. In fact popular shrines sold badges to raise money and some keen travellers had a collection of badges.

Rich local families could pay for their own chapels in the Minster. Here they placed their tombs and daily prayers were said for the family. In the Markenfield Family Chapel, now between the Mother's Union Chapel and St Wilfrid's Chapel, you can still find the life-size stone figures of Sir Thomas, who died in 1398 and his wife Lady Dionisia. Sir Thomas wears medieval armour with a fine sword and a splendid collar showing a stag. He rests his feet on a lion which shows that he was considered a brave knight.

somewhere near the High Altar. Wilfrid's head was kept in the Choir in a special **casket**, maybe gold ornamented with jewels. It was carried around in processions on St Wilfrid's Feast Days. Wilfrid's feet were cut off and displayed separately in the nave, where ordinary people could see them. Nine or more altars were spread around the Minster with precious **alabaster** carvings, many candles and **offertory boxes** for money.

Do as you are told!

The powerful Church ruled the lives of ordinary people and had its own powers to punish wrong doings. Everyone was expected to go to church

on Sundays and Holy Days. In 1468, Joanna, a Ripon woman, was whipped for spinning on a Sunday, when absolutely no work was allowed!

The nave of the Minster had no seats. It was just a large open space where people stood on the stone floor for services. Few people could read or understand the Latin services, so they learnt from pictures instead. Colourful paintings on the walls and the stained glass windows told Bible stories and tales about the lives of the Saints, rather like cartoon strips. In the 14th Century, Robert the **glazier** knew how to use metals and chemicals to make jewel-coloured glass. His little round windows were once in the big window behind the altar. Skilful Medieval **masons** carved strange stone faces such as the Green Man and other grotesques, which amused or frightened people.

Parents brought their babies to be baptised very soon after they were born, just in case they died. In 1439 it cost one halfpenny for a **Baptism**. The baby was lowered completely into a big stone tub *font* full of sanctified water.

People often got sick and died from diseases. During the 12th Century, the Archbishops set up two Hospital chapels in Ripon to provide lodging and food for lepers, blind priests and poor travellers.

Unclean! Unclean!

The Chapel of St Mary Magdalen, also known as The Leper Chapel, had special care for *lepers* and blind priests. Importantly, the chapel and its dormitory buildings were outside the town. Blind priests lived in one lodging house and lepers in another. Lepers were provided with a special garment called a 'bak' and two pairs of shoes each year. Each day they received a loaf of bread and ale, plus meat on meat days and fish on fish days. On St Mary Magdalen's Day, poor people could come to the chapel for a loaf of bread and a herring. Lepers or others with skin diseases were not allowed inside the chapel. Instead, they probably looked through the low side window at services. You can still see this little window. Not surprisingly, people in the town were frightened in case they caught this ugly disease. People

suffering from leprosy probably looked horrible, as their fingers and toes fell off and their faces were eaten away. Lepers had to warn people that they were near, by sounding a clapper or a bell. Leprosy was brought back to Britain from the Holy Land by the Crusaders, but was beginning to decline by the end of the Middle Ages.

The Chapel of St John Baptist provided lodging and simple food, bread and soup, for travellers and poor clerks who taught in Ripon. Poor people asking for alms could have herb or pease soup twice a week.

Ripon needs Neighbourhood Watch

The Middle Ages were dangerous times. Troublesome Scots kept invading the area. They had destroyed Ripon once before, but in 1318 they returned. They demanded 1000 gold coins from frightened townspeople and clergy in Ripon Minster, to save the town from being burned. A wall was built across the East end of the Minster to protect it and the doors fitted with large bolts.

Many people, even clergy, owned weapons. There was a long-standing church law that priests were not allowed to spill blood, nevertheless in 1439, the Archbishop had to remind the Canons that they must not carry swords or daggers under their *cassocks*. The clergy certainly did own weapons, as a Ripon chaplain called Christopher wrote in his Latin will:

"I *bequeath* to William Webster my servant my bow and sword… Also I bequeath to Christopher, son of Roger Warde, one battle axe."

Or, in the original Latin:

"Item lego Willelmo Webster famulo meo, arcum meum, gladium … Item lego Christoforo filio Rogeri Warde, unum batillax."

Note how the English word for 'battle axe' was used.

[Kath Hall]

Activities

Make a casket for St Wilfrid's head or feet

1. Trace the outline of this cube onto shiny gold or silver card and cut it out.

2. Fold it up to make a box.

3. Glue the tabs to keep the cube together but don't glue the top flap which forms the lid.

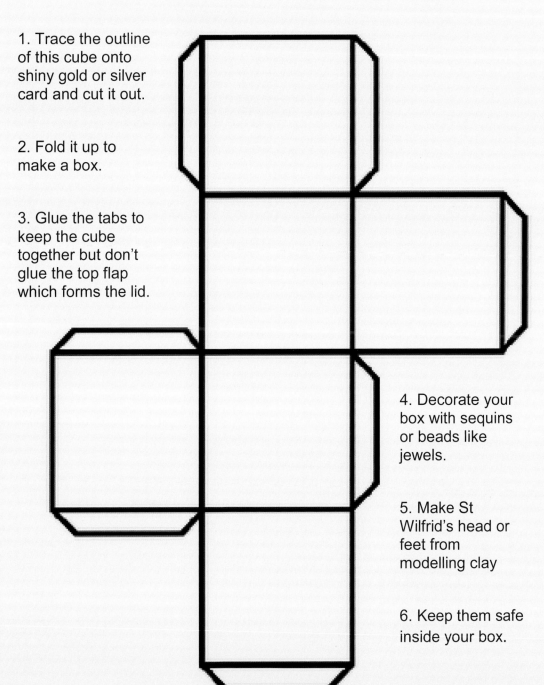

4. Decorate your box with sequins or beads like jewels.

5. Make St Wilfrid's head or feet from modelling clay

6. Keep them safe inside your box.

57

Make your own stained glass window

You need:

- A sheet of black sugar or cartridge paper A3 size
- A piece of transparent sticky backed plastic A4 size
- A piece of card A4 size
- Tissue paper in bright colours
- Scissors with sharp points
- Pencil
- A glue stick

What to do

1. Fold black sugar paper in half to look like A4.

2. Make a card template in the shape of a window slightly smaller than your folded paper.

3. Draw round the template on top of your folded sheet.

4. Through both thicknesses of black paper, cut out the middle window shape, leaving some black edges.

5. *Be careful* not to cut through the outside black edges

6. Open up the folded black paper to show a double frame.

7. Stick the plastic behind the right hand frame, sticky surface upwards.

8. Tear small pieces of coloured tissue.

9. Cover the sticky plastic window shape completely with them.

10. Glue any loose bits down flat.

6. Throw away the middle pieces or use for something else.

7. Fold the left side back, over the right side.

8. Glue the two parts of the frame together.

9. Put your stained glass window over a real window

Let the light stream through!

[Kath Hall]

Chapter 5

The Brass Compasses

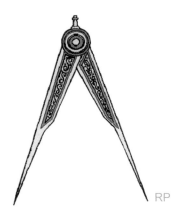

Tilly reached into the chest and her hand grasped something heavy and metallic. 'Ouch! I've pricked my finger on something sharp' she yelled.

'Let me have a look. What is it then?' asked Josh. As he helped her lift the object out, they heard many voices and the clatter of hammers on stone. The twins were holding an old pair of compasses, like the ones they had seen in class, but much bigger and made of brass.

'What is it? Where are we now?' Josh exclaimed, as he realised that they were no longer in front of the old chest.

'Wow!' shouted Tilly above the noise. They found that they were standing at the bottom of a huge building. In every direction, men and young boys were working busily. Some were high up on rickety scaffolding which towered into the sky around half-finished walls. Men dressed in tunics and woolly leggings looked as small as ants as they worked barefoot on the white stone above.

'Look at them. How do they stay up there!' yelled Josh, pointing at men clinging onto the wooden roof as they hammered or laid tiles. It looked impossibly dangerous to them so far below. Gigantic wheels lifted chunks of stone and wood high up the building on ropes that swung dangerously.

'What a racket, Josh, and what **is** that smell?' Tilly said, as she wrinkled her nose. An awful stench rose up from wooden troughs that were full of a horrible looking grey liquid. Everywhere there was noise and bustle. In one place men and boys were hacking stone into plain or carefully decorated blocks. In another area they were sawing and chiselling wood into long beams, others were chipping or painting thick pieces of glass while some better-dressed men just seemed to be shouting orders in loud voices.

'It looks like some sort of huge old building site to me!' Josh replied. Across a field, below the Cathedral, a river glistened and flat boats were arriving piled up with slabs of stone and huge rough logs.

'Watch out below!' yelled a voice from up high. Tilly quickly pushed Josh out of the way as a piece of tile dropped from above, crashing near their feet.

'Phew, that was close!' whistled Josh, 'This place is **really** not safe. And where's their safety gear, some of them haven't even got boots on?' Above them, the outline of the beautiful building was rising into the sky.

'Oi! I've been looking for that,' a muscled man in richly coloured robes shouted as he strode towards the twins. He took the compasses from the Josh's hand. 'I've needed that to measure designs for this 'ere column!'.

'Why, who are you?' asked Josh as he stared at the oddly dressed man. They noticed rolls of drawings in his hand.

'Why, I'm the head mason here at Ripon, of course, working on Archbishop Roger's great project. Don't you know me boy, and why are you not at work? Off you go! Your master will be looking for you and will give you a beating too if you waste any more time!' As the mason walked off, he turned back to face Tilly, 'and what are you doing here girl? The Minster building is no place for girls!'

Tilly opened her mouth to protest, but before she could utter a word, the mason had disappeared and they were back in their own world again.

And now for the facts ...

Dangerous work!

The Normans arrived in England from France in 1066 and quickly began building castles, churches, and cathedrals in stone. In 1174, the Normans began building Ripon minster, as we see it today. This was under the orders of the Archbishop of York, Roger Pont L'Eveque. He was a very important man in England at the time. The growing minster would have been a very noisy, dirty and often dangerous place to work

Many of the tools and methods used would be the same as the ones used today but the scene would have looked very different from a building site now. Some materials were brought to the site but they would still have to be shaped and prepared there. Most things would be made at the site. Blacksmiths and lead workers would be working with red hot metal, carpenters and stonemasons cutting, painters and plasterers mixing, each in their own area around the Minster. Can you imagine building such a massive structure without any power-tools, cranes, lorries or machines? Even today, with all the tools we have, it would be a very difficult job and would take many years!

Look out below!

As well as being excellent craftsmen, medieval minster builders had to be very brave as they took their lives into their own hands every day. They would have had to hang onto roof joists, dodge falling blocks and walk on flimsy wooden scaffolding high above the ground. Pictures of the time show men and boys working in bare feet or leather shoes with no hard hats, goggles or boots! We can imagine that many men and boys must have been killed or badly injured over the years that work went on at the Minster.

Woodcarving in Gloucester Cathedral showing a builder falling from a height

Now lets meet the men who built the Cathedral.

Here comes the Boss!

The most important man at the building of a Minster was the master mason, and he only took orders from the Archbishop. The master mason was the man in charge of all the work and he spent many years learning his trade. He had to draw up plans for the Minster using only compasses, set squares and rulers, and we would now call him an architect. The master mason would have to know how much of each material to order, find out the cost of the work, and get all the men working together, which was often very difficult! The master mason would have been a wealthy and well-respected

HE

Helen Enby

man in the area. In 1359, John of Evesham was paid the huge sum of 3 shillings (15p) per week when he worked on Worcester Cathedral. His work was so good that he was paid for life and was also given a loaf of bread every day!

The big picture!

Often, as well as making paper plans, the master mason would draw up huge maps of the designs on the floor in part of the building. When one part was finished he would rub out the drawings and start again! We know this as York Cathedral still has a "tracing floor". This was left for hundreds of years, and shows how the master mason drew out his designs in chalky powder. At York, there are also medieval templates, (cut out shapes), which the master mason would draw out. He would give these templates to the stonemasons or carpenters to show the shape he wanted cutting and tell them how many were needed of each shape. They would then fit together like a giant model!

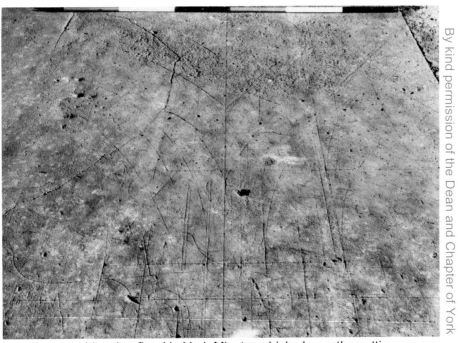

By kind permission of the Dean and Chapter of York

The actual 'tracing floor' in York Minster which shows the cutting patterns for the stonemasons and carpenters to follow.

A chip off the old block!

The stonemasons were the men who shaped, fitted and carved the stone, a very skilled job. A stonemason would usually begin work as a young boy often working with his father. He might start to learn his trade by quarrying stone from the ground, then by cutting rough blocks. After many years, if he worked well enough, he would learn how to carve mouldings (decorated wall carvings) and corbels (stones which support an arch).

A stone corbel

The gruesome gargoyles

The best masons would have carved the scary gargoyles you can see on the outside of the Cathedral. Gargoyles are stone spouts carved into the shape of a mythical beast, such as a griffin, or even a strange human figure, like a "tooth-ache-man". These stick out from the gutter and water pours out of their mouths away from the building (no drain pipes in the Middle Ages). The gargoyles were also thought to ward off bad spirits. The most horrible ones are on the North side of the Cathedral, which was supposed to be the devil's side! They show us the amazing skill of the masons working in Ripon.

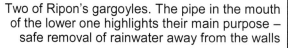

Two of Ripon's gargoyles. The pipe in the mouth of the lower one highlights their main purpose – safe removal of rainwater away from the walls

Leaving your mark!

Although they were very clever at their job, masons could not usually read or write. Many different types of craftsmen would travel around with their tools, moving onto the next place when a building was finished. To show where they had been working, they would often chip a shape or symbol into the blocks of stone they carved. These are called mason's marks and each mason had his own special mark, like a signature. We can see some good examples of these symbols in Ripon Cathedral. Some of the same

A few of the marks made by masons in Ripon Cathedral to identify their work

mason's marks can be seen in different churches, abbeys, and castles in Yorkshire and across the country, which shows us how far they travelled.

Every job had its dangers, and a stonemason might be blinded by flying stone chippings, fall while trying to make blocks fit in high walls or be crushed if a block fell. The tools used to shape the stone and the way it is shaped have changed very little from

HE

? ? ?   **Did You Know**   ? ? ?

It took a stonemason one day to cut one ordinary stone block so it must have taken many days to cut some of the elaborate carvings in Ripon Minster. Imagine sitting all day chipping at one block!

Left: plain hard work would be involved when builders started a project – lifting and carrying by hand or on their shoulders or backs. If pieces were too heavy for one man, others would help.

With bigger items, or when higher heights had to be reached, more mechanical ways had to be found to lift building materials.

Above, from left to right: use of a simple rope pulley, pulley and trolley, pulley and windlass (shaft with handle)

Left: a human treadmill used to tug the rope and a tower with two pulleys and counter-weight to reduce the lift needed.

Drawings: HE

the time the work began on Archbishop Roger's minster as wooden mallets and metal chisels are still used to carve designs. The best medieval stonemasons were paid around 20 deniers a week (or 10 pence). This was around three times the pay of a labourer and shows how skilled they were at their job.

Wood you do this?

To build the Minster, gangs of carpenters, (wood workers), would also come from many miles around. Like other workers, they started by learning to saw and shape simple fittings at a young age and the best would go on to make the finest decorations. In Ripon, we have some large and beautiful bosses that show the carpenter's fantastic skills. These carvings were used to hide the joins in the roof beams. In Ripon, some of the bosses are nearly a metre and a half across and must have taken many weeks to carve. The bosses often show stories from the bible, like the one below showing Adam and Eve being expelled from the Garden of Eden. They were covered in expensive gold leaf (known as gilding), to make them stand out even more. Use the mirrored table in the choir to help you see some of the best bosses in the Cathedral.

Again, carpenters' tools have changed little since Norman times, as chisels, saws and axes are still used in the same way today for fine carving. However, everything would have taken much longer without the power tools used now. The carpenters and stonemasons often worked together. The carpenter would sometimes have to make a practice wooden model of a design that the stonemason wanted to try out, such a new

Ceiling boss in the Choir, showing Adam and Eve being expelled from the garden of Eden

type of arch. The mason could then see if the model would work before making it in stone. This was a lot easier than taking weeks making it in stone, then finding it wouldn't fit together or didn't look right!

What a puzzle

The carpenters would have many jobs on the site such as making doors, religious carvings, window shutters and seating. Another tricky job for the carpenters was to make the window frames. They would have to make huge wooden window frames on the ground, ready to take

HE

? ? ?   **Did You Know**   ? ? ?

Your name might come from what you ancestors did. If your first name was Tom and you worked with wood, you might be called Tom Carpenter or Tom Carver, a blacksmith became Tom Smith, a man who worked the stone often became Tom Mason and Tom Glazier shaped the glass.

the hundreds of pieces of glass and lead. A frame would be fitted into the wall and the glass and lead would then slot in like pieces of a jigsaw. A large window like the huge East Window would need over 100 perfectly shaped pieces of wood. Tom Carpenter would have to choose his wood very carefully; if he picked pieces that would go out of shape, the whole window might fall out!

70

The really dirty work

The labourers were often unskilled peasants who worked for the local church or the richer people who owned the land. The labourers often got the most horrible, hard jobs such as carrying stone and digging foundations. They would also be given the dirtiest jobs such as mixing the mortar. This was very dangerous as mortar contained lime which could strip and burn your skin. It would also be very smelly as they added manure to mortar to help it stick. Some labourers would train in certain jobs, such as cutting the stone into rough blocks and this way they could begin as masons. Life was very difficult as a medieval labourer as you were often poorly treated and poorly paid. Would you do all these disgusting jobs for just 3½ pence (7 deniers) per week?

The stonework inserted in a complex window like the East window in Ripon is called 'tracery'. Its construction required highly skilled carpenters, stonemasons and glaziers

What a pong!

Another very skilful group of people were the glaziers (men who made the stained glass windows). The stained glass must have been a wonderful sight for the people of Ripon, as only the richest people would have glass in

Mixing mortar

HE

71

their homes. The windows would often show stories from the bible or pictures of saints. These would bring light and colour to the Minster. The glazier would have to paint, shape and then fit all the glass pieces together with lead strips. Medieval glass was made in France and was very expensive, so they couldn't afford to make mistakes! The glaziers would have used a dangerous mixture of chemicals to colour the glass including lead and silver oxides, which were both very poisonous. They also used strong urine (wee!) to help the colour dry. Can you imagine the awful smell?

Heavy metal

Also on site would be blacksmiths and lead smiths. These were the men who heated and shaped iron and lead. We know that lead came from Nidderdale and iron came from Fountains Abbey from at least AD 1195. The blacksmiths probably had their own "smithy" or forge on site. They would make all the metal things needed for the building; thousands of nails for the carpenters, the door fittings, locks, even buckets and shovels! The lead smith would make lead for the roof and gutters and for the joins of the leaded windows. In 1393, 1680 pounds of lead (around 800 kilograms) was bought by the Minster!

Glaziers installing a stained glass window

Many other types of craftsmen would be needed to complete the work, including plasterers and painters. It is hard to imagine that the bare stonework we see now was once plastered and decorated with rich colours and beautiful paintings. The only bit of painted plasterwork left is in the Cathedral kitchen. It dates from the 1200s and shows Jesus with his mother, Mary.

How they built it

When we look at a building today, we can usually tell when it was built by its style and how it was made (such as a Victorian house). We need to remember that Ripon Cathedral wasn't really built at any one time. The Cathedral is like a giant model that was built and rebuilt over 500 years and is still changing. Over the years, many parts of the Minster have been burnt, attacked, fallen down or made much bigger! There are many different building styles in the Minster. These styles show us the building fashion of each time. They also show how the ways of working have also changed. In the North transept, for example, we can see how ideas were already changing in 1175. If you look at the wall, you can see both pointed arches, which were in a new style called Gothic, originating in France in the 12th Century. You can also see old Norman style round arches. It looks as though the master mason couldn't make up his mind, so he used both old and new styles!

The medieval recyclers

Some parts of the minster have been rebuilt several times. Instead of knocking down the old building and starting from scratch, the masons would incorporate the original walls. They would also recycle the stone from fallen parts of an older building. This would save them a lot of work!

Travel in time!

To understand how the Cathedral we see today was made, we really need to start around 1174, the time of Archbishop Roger. The new Minster was made three times bigger than the old Saxon church. It was designed to be a smaller version of York Minster. We are very lucky that we can still see much of the building as it was in Archbishop Roger's time. If you stand in the graveyard on the south side of the Cathedral and look at the South

Mixture of round and pointed arches in Ripon Cathedral's north transept

74

transept, you are travelling back in time. The round door and wall that you are looking at are exactly the same as they were over 800 years ago!

Like all Norman Cathedrals and churches, the new Minster was made in the shape of a cross. Work on the new Minster began at the east end, (the end with the large window and high altar). This was so the altar could be fitted as quickly as possible and people could begin to worship in their new building.

From the east end, work would continue down the choir towards the middle of the cross shape. The two parts that come out like the arms of a cross are called the transepts and form the crossing. Above the middle of the crossing rises the central tower. Four fat legs support the tower, which was topped in the 1200s with a tall spire Each leg is joined with arches in between them for strength, like a stool!

Below the arms of the cross is the long nave, which is the main part of the cross shape. The word 'nave' is the Latin word for ship and if you look up at the ceiling of the nave you will see that is shaped like an upside down ship. Archbishop Roger's church didn't have any aisles, (parts separated by pillars), as these were added later but the main part of the nave is the same as it was when built by the Normans.

At the end of the nave is the wonderful west front with its two

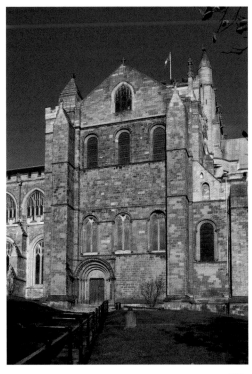

Parts of the south transept, including the doorway, have not changed in over 800 years. Other stonework has had to be replaced. Some recent work is clearly seen in the lighter coloured stone of the large window (left) and some of the higher stonework.

towers. These once had tall spires on top. Work on the West end was completed under the orders of Archbishop Walter De Grey who took over after Roger died.

Nave ceiling

Ouch, my back!

Much of the medieval building work we can see in Ripon Cathedral was done in the same way as castles being built at the same time, like the Tower of London. One of the biggest problems was how to get the stone and wood to the site in the first place. Most of the stone used to build the Norman Minster came from Hackfall quarry, about nine miles away. Some wood came from Scandinavia (where much of our building wood comes from now), but local oak would have been used for rafters, beams and carvings. In 1227, King Henry III gave 30 trees from one of his royal woodlands for work on Ripon Cathedral tower. We believe that stone and wood were floated down by river on barges and then hauled up to the steep hill from the river to the site.

Once there, the next hurdle would be how to get materials to where they needed to be on the site. Even small blocks of stone were too heavy to lift by hand and the men had to use clever ways to get it up to where it needed to be!

The foolish man builds his house on sand

When the Saxons burnt down the old church in 948, the crypt that held St Wilfrid's holy relics was left undamaged as it was underground. Archbishop Roger wanted the crossing of his new church built over this precious crypt. This meant that the East part of the Minster had to be built down a slope and on sandy soil. Imagine what could happen to a huge church built on sand!

The wise man builds his house upon the rock!

To begin the work, gangs of labourers and rough masons dug and lay deep mortar and rough stone foundations for the building. However, the foundations at Ripon were not deep enough for such a large building, especially one built on a slope.

Next, the walls were begun and the carpenters built scaffolding so the masons could build upwards. Scaffolding rose and, as each wall was finished, new foundations were laid and building continued towards the West end.

The walls and columns supporting the Cathedral look strong and solid but they are not in fact as solid as they look! In the 1100s and 1200s, the masons used good stone on the outside but filled the middle with stone chippings and mortar. These walls would have been strong enough for smaller Saxon churches but they were too weak to hold up the high, heavy walls of a huge Norman Minster. All sorts of troubles were in store for the new church.

And the walls came tumbling down!

It wasn't long before problems began. In 1280, most of the East end of the Cathedral came tumbling down! The East end you can see today has a huge and beautifully decorated window which replaces the earlier one. If you look closely above the window, you can see a scar that was left when

The arrows show the scar left by an earlier ceiling which collapsed

the wall collapsed. This shows where the old roof used to be.

The fall also brought down part of the choir and you can find clues in the choir walls to show the problems the builders had when rebuilding. A careful look at the columns in the choir shows that some do not match up.

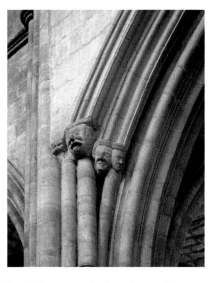

Over the years, there have been other disasters, such as the tower falling down, which you will read about in a later chapter. Different parts of the Cathedral have been strengthened to try to stop disaster happening again. All over the outside of the Cathedral, there are many strong stone supports known as buttresses, especially at the East end. Look and you can see massive buttresses in different styles. These have been added on over the years to prevent the East end falling down the slope again!

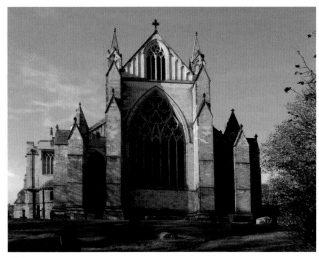

Heavy buttressing supports the East end

Putting in the finishing touches…..

As one bit of stonework was finished, gangs of carpenters would have to make and fit the huge main joists and beams to support the roof. Next, carpenters and plumbers could begin to cover the roof to protect the building from wind and rain so that work could begin on the ceilings inside. We have some amazing ceilings at the Cathedral, both stone and wood which show us how clever the craftsmen were.

We can imagine that many different craftsmen would be putting the finishing touches to the inside of the church at the same time, but actually this might have taken many months or even years. Plasterers and painters would work for months to decorate all the stone and woodwork, and glaziers would delicately fit the glass. Doors and shutters would be made, and statues and woodwork were covered in gold. Silver and gold workers would make metal objects and beautiful fabrics were woven for the altar. The medieval Minster must have looked magnificent!

[Joseph Priestley]

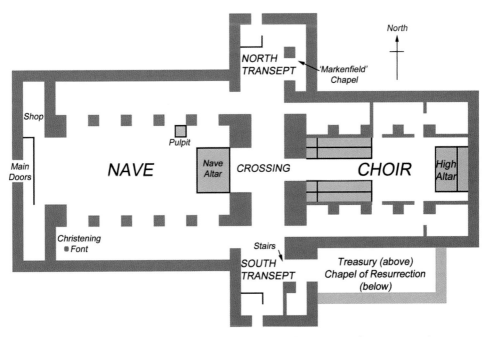

Ripon Cathedral layout today has many of the same features as the stone structure started around the beginning of the thirteenth century

Chapter 6

The Tudor Rose

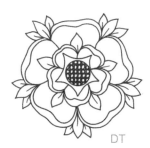

Tilly and Josh couldn't wait to discover what other exciting things they would find in the treasure chest. Tilly decided that she would look inside next. Perhaps there was nothing else to find. What a disappointment that would be.

'I'm going to have the next turn' she said to Josh, pushing him out of the way. She put her hand into the chest and felt around. Her fingers touched something hard and smooth. It seemed to be made of wood and had a kind of pattern carved into it. Tilly carefully lifted the object out of the chest. She held it up to the light so that she could see it clearly. She saw that it was a carved flower.

Josh said 'I've seen something like that before. Isn't it the Yorkshire Rose?'

'No,' said Tilly, 'it's different. I've seen a picture of one like that in a book. I think it is called a Tudor Rose!'

Suddenly the quietness was shattered by the noise of hammering and sawing. People were shouting to each other over the noise. Everything around the twins had changed. They seemed to be standing in a building site. There was dust everywhere. As they watched they saw that the walls on each side of them were being removed and were being replaced by beautiful pointed arches. Josh looked through the archways and he could see men putting something into wheelbarrows. He was curious to see what they had found.

'Just a minute,' he said to himself, 'are those bones?' He was right, for skulls and human skeletons were being piled into the barrows.

'Tilly,' he called. 'Come here!'

She hurried over to see what he had found. Horrified she whispered, 'Josh, what is happening? Are they murderers hiding bodies? I'm scared.'

Before Josh could reply an important-looking man came to the workmen and said, 'Be careful digging up the graveyard. Those skeletons were once people living here in Ripon. All the bones are to be carefully put on shelves in the charnel house for safe keeping.'

'Oh!' said Tilly, 'not murderers after all. Perhaps the men are clearing the ground so that the church can be made wider.'

'Yes,' said Josh, 'I'm going to watch them some more.'

Tilly didn't like the sight of all the skeletons. She felt quite trembly inside at the thought of a room full of them. She wandered towards the other end of the church.

'Plenty of work going on here,' she thought. Men were carrying pieces of carved wood. Tilly was interested. She loved the wooden rose she had found in the chest and wondered what these carvings were and where the men were putting them. What she saw amazed her for she could see that wonderful animals and people had been carved out of solid pieces of wood. She recognised a carving of a rabbit, pigs playing musical instruments and other fantastic animals. Tilly could see a carving of a strong man carrying doors, a man's body sticking out of the mouth of a big fish and many other scenes. Surprisingly, the men were carefully fixing the carvings underneath tip-up wooden seats.

'How odd,' she thought. 'When someone sits on the seat the carvings will be hidden.'

Tilly hurried back to find Josh to tell him about the wonderful carvings, but as she approached him an eerie change came over the scene. All the men stopped working as if frozen to the spot. As the twins watched, a group of men dressed in long black robes walked down the centre of the church. One of the workmen began to move and stepped forward to meet the men. Tilly and Josh could hear angry voices.

'If you can't or won't pay us for our work then we are downing tools and stopping the building work,' the workman shouted.

The men in black tried to explain that the king and the government had taken away the money for the building project and therefore there was no money to give to the builders. All the workmen picked up their tools and silently walked away.

Tilly and Josh were left alone in the empty church and as they looked round it was obvious that the building work had not been completed for two of the biggest arches were partly altered and in some ways the shapes were spoilt.

As they looked at the archway, they saw a group of important-looking people coming towards them. They were dressed in richly embroidered clothes and began pointing at the walls and at some statues.

The children moved nearer so that they could hear the

conversation.

'We have no choice,' one of the men said. 'The law has been changed. There must not be any statues or wall-paintings in the church. All chantry chapels and relics must go. A bible, written in English, must be placed in the church so that anyone can read it. The church building must be undecorated so that everyone can concentrate on the worship of God.'

The children saw the wall-paintings whitewashed over and statues being smashed. The colour and splendour of the church interior was being removed. Tilly hoped that the wonderful wood carvings would be left alone.

'How lucky,' she thought, 'that they are under the seats after all.'

As people went about their work Tilly and Josh noticed two men in long black cloaks move quietly away from the others. The twins crept towards them and saw the men take chisels and sacks from underneath their cloaks. Looking carefully around they quickly began to remove some small statues from the walls and the put them into the sacks.

One of the workmen turned and saw the men. 'Hey, what are you doing?' he shouted. The men stopped and like shadows disappeared into the gloom. The church became empty and silent once more. Then two flickering lights appeared. The twins could see candles carried by the same two men who had taken the statues. The men knelt down and began to dig under the floor. They carefully took the statues from out of the sacks, wrapped them in cloth and put them into the hole they had made. Then they replaced the floor covering and disappeared into the night as silently as they had come.

'I wonder what that was all about?' said the twins together.

'Perhaps we will find out more later,' said Tilly.

And now for the facts ...

The Tudors

The Tudor period was a time of change in England. The population doubled in size and towns grew enormously; London became the largest city in Europe. Law and order improved. People were able to work as merchants and traders as well as on the land. There were more opportunities for education. Boys in particular went to school, working from seven in the morning until five in the afternoon, six days a week. The Church became much less powerful. This was a time of exciting change.

Changes in Ripon Minster (No cash, no work – builders pick up tools and leave)

About 1450 the central tower collapsed causing much damage. It was decided to make the nave of the church wider by removing the walls on the north and south and replacing them with the new style pointed arches. The rebuilding took years because of lack of money and because plague came to Ripon the builders stopped work.

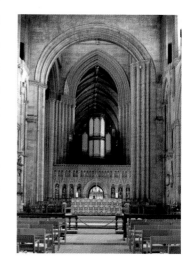

Eventually the rebuild was almost complete when a very important change happened. The king, Henry VIII, made himself the head of the English Church instead of the Pope. No more money was available for building work, so it stopped completely.

Today, the evidence can be seen as two of the large arches are still left in the old, round-headed, style with pillars ready for the pointed arches to be built.

84

A scary problem solved

When the church was widened, the graveyard had to be dug up. Many of the skeletons were removed and placed on shelves in a charnel or bone house. More bones were added as the graveyard became too full. People used to be able to look at the skulls and bones. The bones have now been buried in a big pit in the present graveyard, marked with a plaque.

Bible in every church by royal command

A law was passed in Henry VIII's time that a large bible, written in English, was to be placed in each church so that people could read it for themselves. This was possible because the printing press had been invented, so books did not have to be written by hand. The bible was chained to the lectern so that it could not be stolen. There is a large, modern bible in the church today, which is read from each day.

A little drop of water does you good

Just as today, people were baptised in Tudor times. The Tudor font is still in the church. It has eight sides. Sometimes people did not bring their children into the church to be baptised because Ripon had times of plague. Baptisms took place outside in the fields, far away from the town.

Frontispiece of 1539 bible

Hidden treasures found after hundreds of years

Changes in church worship resulted in the church building being changed too. All statues, wall-paintings and stained glass windows were to be removed. A pulpit was to be placed in the nave with seating for people to sit and listen to the preacher.

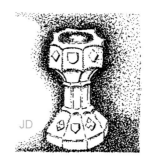

Some of the priests did not like the changes and decided to take some of the alabaster statues and hide them until a safer time. Some were discovered under the floor of the church and are displayed for people to see today.

How fantastic wood can be

From 1489-1494 woodcarvers were busy in Ripon. William Bromflet was the man in charge. He and his team produced beautifully carved choir stalls. They also made some fascinating misericord carvings which were placed underneath the tip-up seats in the choir. A variety of animals, scenes from

Alabaster carving of Christ's resurrection

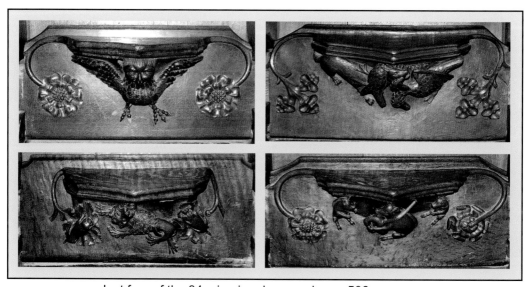

Just four of the 34 misericords carved over 500 years ago

86

bible stories and strange magical animals were carved out of solid pieces of oak. These can be seen today.

Marmaduke, a very wise man

King Henry VIII and his government decided to close down all the abbeys and other religious houses in England. The abbeys and abbots had become too powerful and owned large areas of land. The last abbot of Fountains Abbey was called Marmaduke Bradley. He worked as a priest for part of each year in Ripon Minster and lived at Thorpe Prebend House close by the church. When he became abbot he knew that the abbey was to be closed down and said he would only do the job if he was allowed to return to his house in Ripon. The king's men came to close the abbey on November 26th 1539. Marmaduke gave the abbey up to the king. He then came back to his house in Ripon. He also received a large pension from the king.

The sad journey of a queen

Mary, Queen of Scotland, was Queen Elizabeth I's cousin. Mary wanted to be queen of England as well as Scotland. Elizabeth could not allow this to happen. Mary was therefore imprisoned. She was not put into a prison cell, but she was only allowed to go where Elizabeth agreed. For some time she lived in Castle Bolton in Wensleydale, but was brought to Ripon on her way to travel South, where eventually she was executed.

It is not certain where she stayed in Ripon; however, a letter sent to her cousin, the queen, asks that her son, James, should be looked after and kept safe.

To Queen Elizabeth, from Ripon, 27th January 1568.

Madam, I have never wished to offend you, but I shall take it ill if my child should be delivered up without my consent, by those who have so little right to dispose of him…

[Dorothy Taylor]

Activities

Make a Poesy Mat

A poesy mat was a round earthen-ware plate used for sticky puddings. There was a pattern on one side and on the other side a funny poem or joke was written. When the pudding had been eaten the poesy mat was turned over and the poem or joke was read.

You will need:

- cardboard
- tea plate
- pencil
- felt tip pens
- scissors

1. Place the plate on the card and draw around it. Cut out the circular shape.
2. Using the felt tip pens draw a pattern on one side and write a poem or joke on the other side.

Make a Marchpane (Marzipan) Tudor Rose

In Tudor times people loved sweet things to eat, especially marchpane. It was pressed into wooden moulds and then the patterned shape was taken out and coloured.

You will need:

- a block of marzipan (or modelling clay for anyone with a nut allergy)
- food colouring in red and green
- a small paper plate
- cornflour
- a paint brush
- a blunt knife

1. Cut your marzipan (or clay) into three pieces.
2. Colour one piece red, one green and leave the other one uncoloured.
3. Roll out to about 1cm thick. You may need a bit of cornflour to stop it from sticking.
4. Using the pattern shapes, cut out petals and leaves and make a Tudor Rose on the paper plate. Alternatively you may wish to paint the petals with the food colouring after cutting them out.

[Dorothy Taylor]

Edward's Spectacular Tudor Adventures

A story by pupils at Greystone Community Primary School, year 4

Our story is about Edward Craft who is 9 years old and who lives in Ripon, North Yorkshire.

Edward was a small and clever boy. He loved to play football as a hobby. His mum was called Sarah and his dad was called Rob. Last, but not least, he had a sister called Mary. His best friends were called Sam, Jane and Elizabeth.

He was born in 1560 and his favourite subjects at school were Latin and mathematics.

His teacher, Mr. Holt was the meanest, cruellest person he had ever met. Mr. Holt shouted a lot at Edward; he was not a very happy man!

Edward often got a good whipping- how he wished he had a whipping boy like some of the other children at school!

After it was over, his hand would be as red as the hottest sun.

One day, he was playing football, doing skills. On the way home, he stumbled over a spiky rock. His ball popped and went 'Bang!'. He had hurt his ankle badly and had to limp carefully all the way home.

The year is now 1568 and Edward with his best friend, Sam had run away from school. While he was hopping madly around, trying to put his shoes on properly, he bumped into the night watchman who was around

Ripon town.

The Night watchman!

"What do you think you're doing?", the night watchman growled. "I will inform your teacher about this!"

Edward ran off hurriedly and the boys suddenly heard the jingling of the bells from the market place.

"Ooh, that means the market is open! Let's go!", Edward shouted cheerfully to Sam.

As Edward and Sam walked up Duck Hill to the market place, they looked at each other and grinned.

"Isn't this the life?", they giggled, trying to forget what would happen when they eventually turned up at school.

As they turned into the market place, they heard loud screaming. They broke into a run and as they got nearer, realised that there was a man standing in front of a large crowd. As the axe fell to chop off his hand, Edward realised with horror that the man was Sam's father. Sam burst out crying.

"He wouldn't have stolen anything, honest!", Sam sobbed .

Edward said to Sam, "It will be ok. At least he isn't dead and that is good!".

The next day, Edward ran away from school again because his friend had told him there would be some great bear baiting in the market square. At 12 o'clock, the baiting was on! He quickly ran

with great excitement, heading straight past some old folk and nearly tripping them over. Eventually, he arrived at the market square where he saw the bear baiting! The bear was a giant, grizzly and gloomy.

"WOW! That's a big bear!" shouted Edward nervously.

Edward was a bit scared at first but one minute later, he was picking up a rotten cabbage from the ground and throwing it at the bear. It was getting up on its hind legs and everyone cheered, "BRAVO!".

Just then, everyone gasped as a grand carriage appeared.

The night watchman leant over and said to Edward, "You know who that probably is, boy? That is Mary, Queen of the Scots in her carriage of gold and her big, white steeds. A strong-willed woman she is, escaping her own country because they didn't want her. Hope she doesn't cause any trouble here."

The people of Ripon cheered the Queen and, in her honour, killed the bear in front of her.

The year is now 1570. Edward was having a short break from his labours and decided to play football with his workmate, Henry Trotter, a young boy with dirty brown hair.

"I hope this football doesn't burst because me and my dad made it out of the bladder of the biggest, best pig we killed…it took all night!", boasted Edward.

Edward shot for the goal as hard as he could, carefully aiming for the wide hole. The ball soared through the air and hit the back of a tall, well-dressed, thin man wearing a top hat the colour of night. The man angrily turned around and shook his fist at the two boys. To the boys' horror, he slowly and slyly walked towards them. A shudder went down Edward's spine. He crossed his fingers behind his back and hoped the man would not hurt him.

"You're coming with me, boy!", shouted the man in anger and grabbed Edward by the scruff of the neck. "I said, you're coming with me!", repeated the spooky, creepy man.

He dragged Edward through the market place and on to Gallows Hill. Edward gasped at all the people being hanged. Some he knew, some he liked the look of, some that were complete strangers.

"This is what will happen to you if you do that again, you little beast!", threatened the man. Edward nodded and spluttered a quick apology before the man let him go. Edward looked around in relief as he saw Henry had followed them. Henry's eyes were staring with horror at the scene in front of him.

"All those people…what are they being hanged for?" asked Edward to a man standing nearby.

"Haven't you heard of the Rising of the North, boy? All these people

were involved. That Mary, Queen of Scots, is trouble," he replied knowingly.

The following day, Edward found himself at the large church that stood near Kirkgate. He looked up in awe.

93

This was a huge, grand building. His Aunt Marge was having her baby christened at the beautiful stone font just inside the front doors.

Edward waited patiently.

"What's this one called, Auntie?" Edward asked, excitedly.

"Jacob. Oh, this has been my sixth baby now and I am getting so tired. He wakes me up so early in the morning!" she sighed.

As Edward laid his head on the stone of the font, his mind drifted back to what he had seen yesterday. To see all those people hanging there had made him feel guilty. Why had these people have to die just for what they believed in?

Edward turned around and prayed for their souls quietly.

Later on that night, after they had all returned home, their neighbour called in to tell them that the night watchman was doing his rounds.

"Please, Auntie, let us pay the night watchman to watch our house. It will only cost 2 pennies per door and I feel anxious tonight", Edward pleaded.

"I suppose we could do that for a while" agreed his aunt. "It will certainly make me feel happier knowing our doors are watched through the night until dawn, especially with such strange happenings in the town lately."

As Edward snuggled into bed that night, he thought about school tomorrow. Mr. Holt was going to be furious. Unless Edward went on some more adventures, of course!

Chapter 7

King James

DM

The Silver Spur

Excitedly, Josh and Tilly looked into the chest and saw a silver spur. They knew this was for a horse rider to put on the heel of his boot. They had learnt in class that Ripon used to be famous for the manufacture of rowels, the round spiked part used to prod a horse if needed. Josh took the spur out of the chest.

Tilly said, 'I want one too' when she saw another spur, which she grabbed quickly. The children looked at the Minster wall. The nearly perfect stones had changed and now looked in bad shape and Josh even managed to put his hand into a big hole in part of the wall. The whole building had damp walls and needed repair.

Josh whispered, 'this looks dreadful!'

All of a sudden they heard people talking loudly, so they hid behind a pillar. Just as they managed to dive for cover, a group of strangely dressed men and elegant ladies appeared. The men had pointed beards and moustaches and their hair was collar length. They wore capes and breeches. The ladies were wearing long silk dresses and had their hair arranged high on their heads.

One of the men seemed to be important and Tilly heard him being called 'Your Royal Highness,' which let her know this was the King.

'Let's follow them to see what they do and where they go,' whispered Tilly.

After some time of serious talking about the repairs which had been done and which needed to be done, the group filed out of the Minster and walked to a house nearby. Again, the children followed, carefully keeping out of sight. When the people had entered the house, the twins sneakily looked through the open door of the house.

'Look at that food!' Josh murmured as his eyes opened wide.

There, a huge table was set out with food. Josh felt hungry when he saw the platters of roast mutton, chicken and beef, as well as breads, salad, apple desserts and other puddings. Each person filled a plate with food, sat down to eat, and when they wanted to have more food, they stood up and filled their plates again and sat down at another place at the table. Josh and Tilly could see the King was being entertained well by the citizens of Ripon and one of them even recited a poem:

'From every place (good king) see how they run

To feast their eyes, and cry – 'He's Com! He's Com!'

The King was then given a pair of silver spurs as a memento of his visit to Ripon Minster and town.

This was when Josh and Tilly discovered they no longer held the spurs in their hands and found themselves back in the Cathedral, which looked in a good state of repair once more.

And now for the facts ...

King James I

ing James I was important to the history of Ripon. It has been said that James was pleased with the treatment by the townsfolk of his mother, Mary, Queen of Scots when she visited Ripon.

Countries Unite!

King James I was the first Stuart King of England. He was descended from King Henry VII, who was the first Tudor King. His mother was the famous Mary Queen of Scots who was forced to give up her throne in Scotland when some people thought she had plotted the murder of her husband.

When his mother was thought to be unsuitable as queen in 1567, James, at the age of 13 months, became King James VI of Scotland. James had had a strange childhood as he had been taken away from his mother at this time and brought up by different nobles in Scotland. He never saw his mother again.

His mother was kept a prisoner at several places in England, including nearby Bolton Castle and Ripon. She was later beheaded by order of her cousin Queen Elizabeth I of England. This was because Elizabeth had been told that Mary had planned to have her murdered.

In 1603, when Elizabeth died childless, James became King James I of England while continuing as James VI of Scotland. He was 37 years old and had 3 children of his own.

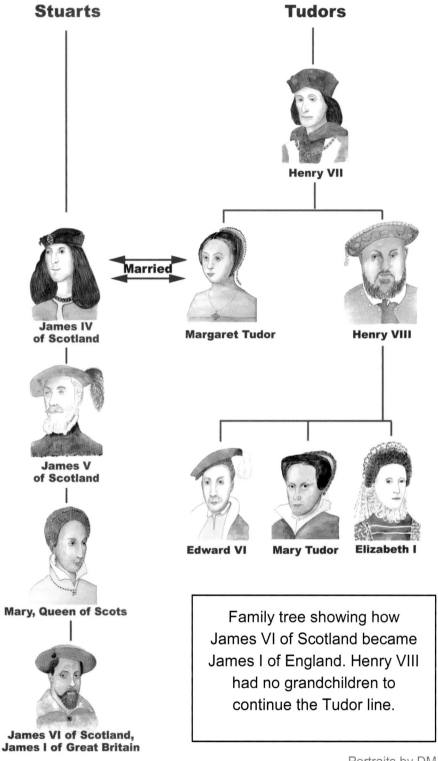

Stuarts

Tudors

Henry VII

James IV
of Scotland

◄━ **Married** ━►

Margaret Tudor

Henry VIII

James V
of Scotland

Edward VI   Mary Tudor   Elizabeth I

Mary, Queen of Scots

James VI of Scotland,
James I of Great Britain

Family tree showing how
James VI of Scotland became
James I of England. Henry VIII
had no grandchildren to
continue the Tudor line.

Portraits by DM

New King makes changes!

In order to tell the people how important they were, the monarchy always used symbols such as flags and coats of arms to give out the messages they wanted people to hear. This began in the Middle Ages when heraldry was important in battle, so that the knights knew who was a friend or foe. In those days there was no TV or Internet which they could use for publicity!

When James became the King of England as well as Scotland, one of the first things he did was to change the English coat of arms by removing the Welsh dragon and putting the Scottish unicorn opposite the English lion rampant. It was very important that everyone knew that England and Scotland were ruled by the same king for the first time ever. The unicorn was chosen because it was a symbol of unity - instead of having two separate horns like most animals, the horns are twisted together to make one. It seems most likely that the Unicorn Hotel on Ripon Market Place was named in honour of James, because the oldest record of it was in 1625 after he had visited the city in 1617.

Left: James I coat of arms (as seen on Ripon's Charter of 1604)

Right: the façade of the Unicorn Hotel, 2010

99

James I also had the first union flag designed to show that Scotland and England were now one. The first known sketches of some of these designs are shown here.

Ripon seeks Royal Help

In 1603 the Cathedral had been short of money for so long that bits of it were falling down. It was in such a bad state that a letter of the time describes the stone walls as having holes in them. There wasn't money to pay enough clergymen, so there was only one person called Moses Fowler to minister to all the people in Ripon.

This oil painting at Ripon Cathedral, shows James I, his wife and one of his sons

Hugh Ripley was the Wakeman of Ripon at the time and he and Moses Fowler worked very hard to persuade the new King James I to give them some money to repair the church, to pay for more clergymen and to make the town more important.

Of course, all this was centuries before the invention of telephones or email! Moses Fowler and Hugh Ripley had to follow the King around the country and buy expensive gifts for his wife and closest advisors before they could even get to meet with him. Eventually, they were successful, and the King granted Ripon two charters in 1604.

A charter is the monarch's instructions put into writing. The picture shows

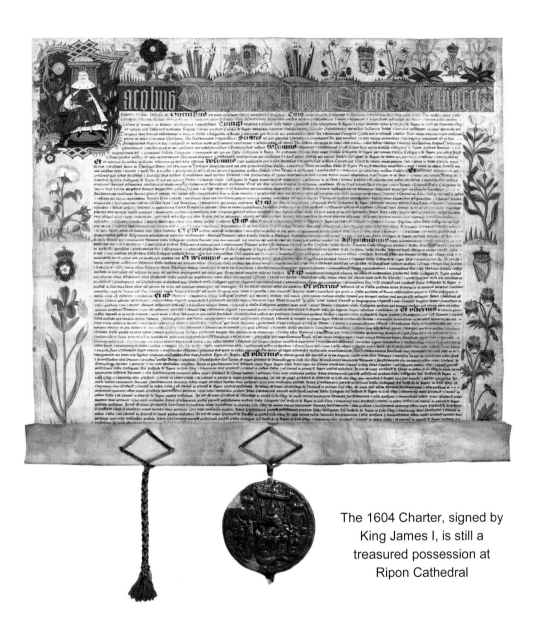

The 1604 Charter, signed by King James I, is still a treasured possession at Ripon Cathedral

A small part of the Latin wording in the charter above. Can you see the name 'Moses Fowler'?

the charter handwritten in Latin on parchment (fine animal skin).

The first church charter made Moses Fowler the first Dean of the Cathedral in 1604, and in the same year Hugh Ripley became the first Mayor of Ripon. James would have granted this charter as he wanted the people of Ripon to be grateful and loyal to him.

The charter promised that money would be given to improve the church buildings. But, some of the rich people James had expected to pay for this were not very happy about it, and two more charters had to be written before all the money was paid.

Death Threat

"Remember, remember, the fifth of November

Gunpowder, treason and plot

I see no reason why gunpowder, treason

Should ever be forgot."

When James I was King of England, there were very strong and sometimes violent feelings about who should be on the throne. One failed plot against the king is still remembered by us all on bonfire night! On 5th November 1605 a gang of men were ready to ignite the barrels of gunpowder which they had hidden in a cellar underneath where King James was due to sit in Parliament. They were found and arrested before they set off the explosion. Several of the men arrested were from the Ripon area. One of the local

DM

plotters, Thomas Percy, was married within the parish of Ripon, but the most famous was Guy Fawkes who came from Scotton near Knaresborough. Guy Fawkes was sentenced to death for treason and was hung, drawn and quartered in London. He was not burnt at the stake as people might think when they see the "guy" on the bonfire every November!

New Conquests

During the reign of James, there was much exploration of the world. This was when the first adventurers from England sailed over the Atlantic Ocean to try to set up a new life in America. The settlement of Jamestown, in what is now the state of Virginia, was called after King James. Pocahontas, the daughter of a native American who had helped the settlers, married an Englishman. She visited England where she met King James.

[Moira Stalker]

Portrait of King James I

from the 1604 Charter

Activities

Design a coat of arms

King James chose a lion and a unicorn for his new coat of arms. Which symbols and colours would you choose for one for yourself?

Design a new flag for the city of Ripon or even one for Ripon Cathedral.

Can you fix this word?

Rearrange the letters: **HNOPCTSAOA**

to find the name of someone who brought ideas from the New World to the King's court

Look for two statues of King James in the Cathedral

(hint: you can see both from the same place, but you will have to look up as well as across)

Look for the memorials to Moses Fowler and Hugh Ripley in the Cathedral

(ask a guide if you need help)

Listen to the Hornblower in Market Square

The Hornblower sounded the setting of the time when the Wakeman became responsible for the safety of the people of Ripon. Even now, the Hornblower blows the horn in the Market Square every evening. Find out what time he plays and go along.

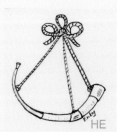

[Moira Stalker]

Chapter 8

England Upside Down

(The Civil War - 1642 to 1649)

Charles I : Still with his head-but not thinking straight!

 n 1625 Charles I became King. He thought that God had chosen him to rule and hid his shy, nervous character by acting strong. His marriage to Henrietta Maria, a French *Roman Catholic* princess, was unpopular. Charles soon quarrelled with *Parliament* over money and religion.

King Charles

Parliament tried to control the King by limiting his money and sacking his favourite advisor, George Villiers, 1st Duke of Buckingham. Charles angrily responded by dismissing Parliament and ruling without them.

Royal Rule: Who needs MPs anyway?

King Charles raised money by making new taxes. Also he tried to control the **Presbyterian** church of Scotland by introducing Bishops and **Anglican** worship. When he made the Scots use a Book of Common Prayer they rioted and the First Bishops War began.

Bishops Wars: No, they didn't actually fight but the Scots did!

Charles' army was poorly trained and no match for the better Scottish army. Neither side really wanted to fight and Charles agreed to let the Scots sort out the problems. This resulted in the Scots freeing themselves from the Bishops and Charles' rule.

In the long run this did not work out and Charles wanted to defeat the Scots. For this he needed more money and had to recall Parliament in 1640. The demands of the Members of Parliament (MPs) were too much for Charles and again Parliament was dismissed. Charles had to fight without Parliament's help.

This time the highly organised and motivated Scottish army soon defeated the Royal army. They invaded Northern England and took over two counties (Northumberland and Durham). Once more Charles had to agree to the Scots' demands but this time the terms of peace were embarrassing. The peace *treaty* was signed in Ripon. Although York was originally planned for the meeting, fear of York's plague made Ripon the better meeting place.

? ? ?   Did You Know   ? ? ?

£850 is worth £130,000 in today's money !

Treaty of Ripon: And Ripon wasn't even fighting anyone!

The Treaty of Ripon was a major setback for Charles. It stated that the two counties in Northern England had to be left in Scottish hands. This was until payment was made to the Scots for their War

expenses. Can you imagine, the Scots demanded that their armies be paid £850 per day to stay in the English counties? The talks lasted over a year and took place in one of the *prebendal* houses in Ripon. The house is no longer standing but a wall plaque in Low St Agnesgate marks the place.

The Treaty of Ripon forced Charles to recall Parliament and agree to the MPs' conditions. The MPs passed laws to control the king. One law said Parliament could not be sacked without its own agreement. Eventually, in 1642, Charles stormed into Parliament with an armed guard. He wanted to arrest five of the leading MPs but they had been warned and had escaped.

Civil War: Mostly it was very un-civil!

The same year Charles declared War on Parliament and left London to rally support. He travelled north to raise an army while Parliament asked their followers to help fight the King. The Civil War had started and people of England had to decide whether to support the King or Parliament. Some families were divided and had relatives fighting on both sides.

Officers in the King's army were called *Cavaliers*. They liked to dress fashionably and wear feathers in their hats.

HE

Those supporting the King were mainly great landowners in the North and West. They were often Catholic and Ripon and the surrounding areas were strong Royalist areas.

King Charles I and his men

107

The soldiers in the Parliament's army were called **Roundheads**.

Roundhead helmet

Supporters of Parliament were usually wealthy people living in big cities. They hated the King's taxes. The **Puritans** too, hated the King because he would bring back the Roman Catholic religion.

Sir Thomas Mauleverer: An ungrateful man who liked his churches plain

Thomas Mauleverer was born into a very old Yorkshire family who owned a lot of land. He was knighted by Charles I twelve years before the Civil War but had to pay for the title! Sir Thomas was made an MP for

Boroughbridge. The King made him a baronet, a year before the Civil War, in an effort to have him as a Royalist. Mauleverer repaid him by raising his own army against the King! These troops became well known for raiding churches, stealing and damaging their contents. Mauleverer's troops joined Sir Thomas Fairfax's attacks on many northern Royalist strongholds.

Damage to Ripon Minster: Chaos in the Cathedral

In 1643 Mauleverer rode to Ripon

Memorials in the Cathedral believed to have been damaged by Roundheads

after he failed to capture Skipton Castle. The Castle had been defended by a brilliant soldier called Sir John Mallory.

Mauleverer hated losing! He and his men entered the Minster. They shattered the magnificent great East window and damaged other medieval glass.

The memorials of Dean Moses Fowler, Sir Thomas Markenfield and Dean Anthony Higgin are thought to have been damaged at this time.

Ripon and the Minster were rescued by Sir John Mallory. Mallory was joined by other men faithful to Ripon. They came across the rebels who had

Memorial in Ripon Cathedral to Sir John Mallory (sometimes spelled 'Mallorie')

? ? ?   **Did You Know**   ? ? ?

Many soldiers injured in the fighting later died from infection or loss of blood.

positioned themselves in the Market Place. Taken by surprise the rebels were defeated by Mallory's men and "made to feel the sharpness of their swords". Some were taken prisoners and sent back to Skipton and other places.

It was many years before the damage to the Minster was repaired.

The New Model Army: Not Toy Soldiers!

After a number of battles Parliament created a strong fighting force called the New Model Army. In this army an officer was chosen for his skills and not because his family was rich and important. The commander-in-chief was Sir Thomas Fairfax and Oliver Cromwell was in charge of the cavalry.

The Royalists lost more and more battles against Cromwell's cavalry. Cromwell's officers studied the best way to attack the enemy. Their uniform gave them good protection but was light for the horses. This gave the horses a faster pace and normally surprised the Royalists.

? ? ?   Did You Know   ? ? ?

Local family acts as eye witness

The earliest known owners of the Unicorn are Edward Turner and Margaret Allanson. They married at the beginning of the 17ᵗʰ century. Edward died after 20 years of marriage but Margaret continued to run the hotel for another 23 years. Margaret saw a number of troubled times for Ripon. At the beginning of Charles I's rule Ripon was in the grip of a severe plague. Did Margaret see the fighting in the Market Place between Mauleverer's troops and Mallory's men?

Margaret finally died in 1647, after the King was a prisoner in Ripon. What did she feel about the King being a prisoner in Ripon?

The King a Prisoner: The King who would not give up!

The Royalists army could not defeat the New Model Army. After escaping from a major battle in Oxford, the King surrendered to the Scottish **Presbyterian** army. The Scottish army finally agreed to deliver the King to Parliament. On his way to London the King spent two days as a prisoner in Ripon.

When Charles was a prisoner in London he managed to escape. He tried to bargain with the Scots. This resulted in the second Civil War with Charles and the Scots invading England. The Royalists had risen again in July 1648.

National Portrait Gallery, London

Oliver Cromwell

Oliver Cromwell: He liked Ripon so much he visited it twice!

In August 1648 Oliver Cromwell was on his way to battle at Preston and stopped in Ripon. He is thought to have stayed

1642, October

1645, June

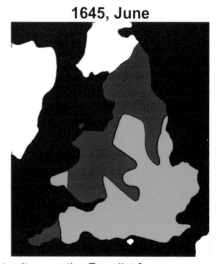

Royalists

Parliamentarians

The maps show the changing control of English territory as the Royalist forces were defeated by the Parliamentarian army during the Civil War

overnight at the Unicorn Hotel.

Oliver Cromwell once again visited Ripon in 1651 while travelling from Scotland to battle in Worcester. He must have enjoyed this visit as he later granted Ripon the right to have a fair every other week!

Cromwell's second visit to Ripon was two years after Charles I was beheaded. Cromwell was one of the 59 MPs (the **regicides**) who signed the King's death warrant. By now the army had great power and Cromwell believed there would never be peace until the King was dead. Sir Thomas Mauleverer and Sir John Bourchier also signed the death warrant.

Sir John Bourchier: A man of no regrets!

Sir John Bourchier, a local landowner, became an enemy of Charles I by refusing to pay him money. He was also heavily fined after arguing with the Council of the North over land. At the start of the Civil War he was arrested and put in prison at York. He was later freed and within a year joined forces with Parliament against the King. Four years later he became MP for Ripon and continued this role after the King was executed.

Beningbrough Hall is now on the site of Sir John Bourchier's original home

> ? ? ? **Did You Know** ? ? ?
>
> Boys caught playing football on a Sunday could be whipped as a punishment.

He never thought his action of signing the King's death warrant was wrong. On his death bed he said, "I tell you it was a just act: God and all men will own it."

The Commonwealth: What, no Royal family?

Following Charles I's execution Britain became a republic called the **Commonwealth**. The Commonwealth was ruled by Oliver Cromwell and Parliament. Parliament would not agree to new elections. Cromwell, supported by the army, sacked the MPs and ruled himself! He was crowned as Lord Protector at Westminster Abbey, even sitting on Charles I's throne!

Life in Ripon: Tough times for everyone

Cromwell was a Puritan and believed he was an instrument of God. He was very religious and thought everyone should live according to the strictest rules in the bible.

A Puritan couple

Ripon men and women were told they had to lead good, simple lives. Children had to be very obedient and parents were encouraged to be very strict. This meant many forms of entertainment were banned. Inns and theatres were closed down. Laws were passed against many sports, dancing, card playing and swearing. What do you think they did for fun?

Sunday became a special day where most forms of work were banned. Even going for a walk, unless it was to church, could lead to a large fine. Instead of having feast days to celebrate the saints, one day in every month was a fast day. This meant

113

no eating all day! Christmas celebrations were stopped. Cromwell believed people ate and drank too much rather than thinking about the birth of Jesus.

Women and girls had to wear long black dresses covering them from the neck to the toes. Their hair was bunched up and hidden by a head-dress. No bright colours or make-up were allowed. Puritan leaders and soldiers walked the streets and scrubbed off any make-up found on women.

Men also wore black clothes and had short hair.

Worship in Ripon: Same church; different services and all very confusing

Charles I had made many changes in the church. He started Catholic-style Bishops and replaced bible study with prayer books. A law had been passed ordering everyone to go to church services. This law was really aimed at the Puritans who disliked the Roman Catholic church.

Altar rail – to stop dogs?

People went to church less and less. There was even cock fighting inside them! Rails were used to stop dogs going onto the altar. Some time before Charles I was beheaded, church services had already stopped in the Minster.

Oliver Cromwell had a deep hatred of the Roman Catholic church. He overturned the changes made by Charles I. The Book of Common Prayer and all service books were replaced with a Directory of Public Worship.

Catholic vestments were colourful

114

Bishops disappeared and Deans were replaced with "preaching ministers". The pulpit became more important than the altar. The sacraments were banned and all Roman Catholic pictures and statues of saints were removed from the Minster.

The "preaching ministers" wore plain gowns and not decorated robes.

HE

This type of worship was practised until Charles II was made King in 1660. In this year the centre spire of the Minster crashed down in a storm!

[Arlene Coulson]

JD

Sketch of cathedral west front
before the collapse

115

Activities

Bashed heads

Several memorials were smashed during the Civil War and some have still not been repaired.

Dean Higgin had left all his books to the Cathedral. Where do you think his memorial might be?

Tomb Raiders

The Markenfield tomb also was damaged. Can you find it? What is strange about Lady Dionysia's feet? Ask a Cathedral guide to check the answer.

Smashed Windows

The broken pieces of glass from the large East window were kept and put together to form a new window in the South Nave Aisle. There is a little dog in this window. Can you find it?

[Arlene Coulson]

116

Chapter 9

Lightning Strikes

It began to rain as Josh and Tilly walked home from school. Then the wind grew stronger and the thunder started.

'One, two, three, four,' counted Josh as another flash of lightning streaked across the sky. 'It's four miles away, heading this way. Quick Tilly, we'll shelter in the Cathedral,' and they began to run. At the Cathedral entrance they leant upon the heavy wooden door which gradually opened. They tumbled inside, giggling and shaking their coats.

As they quietly walked through the Cathedral into the Choir, Tilly began to text their Mother to let her know that they were safe. Suddenly there was a strong flash of lightning inside the Cathedral.

'Josh!' cried Tilly. 'It's happening again. We're wearing peculiar clothes. We're travelling back in time. My mobile's disappeared.' The loud crash from the roof above the Choir stalls made them look up.

'Quick, run,' yelled Josh, 'the roof's falling in.'

'Josh, Josh, run run run,' screamed Tilly. 'Hide behind the wooden seats.' Then she couldn't see her brother anywhere.

'Where are you, Josh?' Tilly's anguished cry echoed throughout the Cathedral which had strangely changed back into a much older building. 'Josh,' she yelled, 'the big spire is falling through the roof. Look up at the ceiling. The wooden spike, it's crashing into the Choir stalls. We must have flown back to 1660. Are you safe, Josh? Answer me please.'

There was no reply. Huddled low, Tilly watched the collapsing roof above her as the storm grew stronger, wind lashing the rain in all directions. She covered her ears as, with a dreadful crash, another enormous hole appeared in the roof. The falling spire splintered the roof into a million pieces sounding like canon fire shooting from a thousand guns. Lightning flashed, inside and out, as rain cascaded down like Niagara Falls. The spire was heading for the wooden seat where Tilly cowered and she screamed.

'Josh, Josh, where are you? I'm scared?' She lay huddled in the dark, moaning and shivering, tears streaming down her face as the wooden spire came crashing down towards her …

'Wakey, wakey, lazy bones. It's time to get up. Josh!! Tilly!! You'll be late for school. Come on!!' A loud groaning came from the children's bedrooms as they dragged themselves out of bed and reluctantly washed and dressed.

'Josh,' whispered Tilly, 'I had such a strange dream. I lost you in the Minster in a thunder storm and the…'

'Tilly, it wasn't a dream, shhhhhh don't let Mummy hear. I was there but you couldn't hear me because of the storm. It was magic, Tilly. True magic. We are the Time Travel Twins, Tilly! What an adventure. I'm going to write about it at school. They'll never believe us, never!!'

And now for the facts ...

Hand, a Fox & Oops-a-Daisy

uring the years **1660-1836** many people worked on or in Ripon Minster or were buried here. Some have very interesting stories to tell:

1660 – A bad penny and some bodwells

'I am James. My father, Thomas Cartwright, came home and told me the central spire of Ripon Minster has collapsed in a storm and fallen through the roof of the choir stalls. King Charles II has said yes to money being collected to repair the roof. Money given has included a bad penny and several bodwells. (A bodwell was a Scottish copper coin worth about one-sixth of an English penny). But the workmen are happy with the ale they are given during the work. Our new dean, Dr John Wilkins, will give support to the ruling power of the country. Dr Wilkins is polite, charming and much liked by everyone.'

1662 - Wave to the hand

'My name is Richard Tullie and I am fourteen years old. I am sitting in my seat in the choir stalls of Ripon Minster, together with my friends. The service has begun and I am about to sing. We cannot see the organist but it is fun keeping time by watching the wooden hand wave up and down. I am waving back but no-one can see me. My father says it is good to have a choir again after so many years. During the Commonwealth when

Oliver Cromwell ruled, prayer and music books and organs were destroyed and all the choirs were banned. The dean of the Minster is called John Wilkins. He has married Oliver Cromwell's youngest sister. As well as that, he believes that one day men might fly but that no-one will ever live on the moon. Why should you want to live on the moon? It is a very long way away and how would you get there? Now in 1662 festivals have started again, the organ, glass windows and tombstones are being repaired. The new organ will be one of the sweetest sounding in the kingdom.'

1663 – Hanged, drawn and quartered

'My name is Eliza. I worship at Ripon Minster. The land is getting more festive since the end of the Commonwealth but people are still disagreeing about religion. I heard that the Baptist John Bunyan and some Quakers were put in prison for what they believe.

Recently there was a lot of trouble. Dr Richardson talked to us at Ripon Minster; he used to be a preacher here. We thought he was a good man but he has been plotting against the Government. "The Farnley Wood Plot" was discovered by King Charles II's soldiers and prisoners were taken. My father says that if they are found guilty they will be hanged, drawn and quartered.

Dr Richardson was lucky to escape.'

1664 – Oops-a-daisy

'Jane Townley is my name. Four years ago the central spire of Ripon

Helen Enty

Minster fell down in a storm. Now, just to be safe, the two, tall wooden spires, which are still on the roof, are being taken down by my uncle Matthew Townley. Uncle Matt is a very brave man and climbs up high buildings. But he has had a terrible fall. He was taking down one of the wooden spires and was at the top of the spire tied by ropes held by workmen below. Uncle Matt was not thinking about what he was doing. Instead he was watching two horses racing on Bondgate Green. The losing rider was holding his horse back and Uncle Matt shouted out "Let go, let go". But the boneheaded workmen thought he meant them and let go of the ropes. Uncle fell from the spire to the tower. He is exceedingly sore in body and temper.'

1696 – Mind your manners, Thomas Umpleby

'I'm George. My neighbour, Thomas Umpleby, is a singing man in the

Minster. He has been told off for not minding his manners. He has been warned that he will be banned if he does not behave in a more orderly way. He must get down on his knees to say he is sorry and also take 40 shillings less in his pay. Next year his usual pay of £8 per year will be restored, if he is good! My mother says she doubts he can be good for long!"

1717 – How many wives?!

'I am a very wealthy man and my name is Sir Edward Blackett. My life has been very busy with building and marrying. Not one wife, not two wives … but three! Do not worry - I only had one wife at a time. My first wife, Mary, gave me a son who died as a child. Then my wife died. I remarried and my second wife, another Mary, had twelve children (six boys and six girls). In 1689 I was returned as a Member of Parliament (MP) for Ripon. The same year I bought the Newby Estate from members of the Crosland family. I did not like the way the house was set out so I had it rebuilt in the 1690s and made it into a very fine house indeed. In 1699 my second wife died. So I married again but wife number three, Diana, died too, in 1713. I have ordered my memorial and am helping with the design.'

1718 – Rest in peace

'My father, Sir Edward Blackett, has died this year of 1718. He was 69 years of age. I am one of his daughters, Henrietta-Maria. The family memorial shows  my father relaxed and comfortable lying centre front with two of his wives standing either side of him.'

1721 – The First Obelisk

'I live in Ripon and my name is Isabella Harcourt. I am 12 years old. Over the years there have been some bad goings-on in the Government. My mother has told me that a Member of Parliament (MP) for Ripon called John Aislabie was put in prison in the Tower of London. Yet

members of the Aislabie family have been MPs for Ripon since 1695. The South Sea Bubble was something to do with financial speculation (risky dealings with money), ship trading rights and the slave trade. But it all went wrong and the MPs quickly sold off their shares leaving other people in the country to pay the debts. When John Aislabie came out of prison he went back to his estate at Studley near Ripon and gardened. His son, William, bought Fountains Abbey which was added to Studley Gardens. The obelisk in the Market Square in Ripon was provided by John Aislabie in 1702. It was the first obelisk in England.'

1752 – Confused and perplexed

'We were perplexed. Before England changed the Julian calendar to one called Gregorian this year, we had two ways of keeping dates. According to the legal and church calendars the year started on March 25th, however, the festival of New Year was celebrated on January 1st. My great-grandmother Hellen Bayne died on March 24th and the old New Year started on March 25th. So, on my grandmother's plaque in the Cathedral it says she died in 1694/1695. It was a confusion to us all at the time – and I suppose still is to me.'

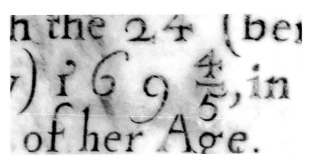

1783 – Do as you would be done by

'My father Robert Porteus owned a tobacco plantation in Virginia which was worked by slaves. Later in life he lived near Ripon and has a memorial in the Minster. I am Bishop Beilby Porteus and I spoke against the practice of slavery in Parliament even though some of my relatives own estates in America and Barbados which are worked by slaves.'

1818 – Water, water

'I am Commander John Elliott, R.N. (Royal Navy) My life has been exciting in many ways. What I really wanted was to be captain of a warship but this did not happen. However, at the age of about thirteen I joined Captain James Cook's 1772-5 voyage around the world – this was the second such trip. I wrote about it and also about the eleven battles which I endured during my life in the Navy. My skills at navigating (finding the way) and mapping were praised by the officers above me. Although I fought duels and quarrelled with my family I was "cool, firm and collected" on the ships. Unlike many sailors I drank only water. I have now retired to live in a house named Elliot House which I built in Ripon.'

1819 – Not a happy chappy

'My name is Henry George Liddell and I am eight years old. Later in my life I marry and one of my ten children will be named Alice. The book

called "Alice's Adventures in Wonderland" will be written for her by Lewis Carroll whose real name is Reverend Charles Lutwidge Dodgson. But that is a long time in the future.

At the moment I am very unhappy. I have been sent to

A caricature of Henry George Liddell in Vanity Fair magazine, 1875

124

Mr Pickersgill's School at Bishopton Grove near Ripon. I will be here for four years and I am miserable. At least the cobblestones in Ripon Market Place are better than they were. The cows at the market made a terrible mess and the smell was unbearable. Now the ground has been covered in something called concrete which is smoother and easier to clean. I have been told that Ripon has a very good cricket club. If I am a good boy I might be able to watch them play. But I just want to go home.'

1830-34- Tick tock

'Hello again. Commander John Elliot here to tell you about the state of the Minster. I am nearing the end of my life now but I wanted you to know that in the last few years parts of the Minster had to be mended because it had

HE

not been cared for. One of the deans left the church-money in a muddle before he went to a different country. Another dean spent much time in Spain pretending he was researching. Despite that I think that the first outside dial clock is still working well since it was put on the South West tower of the Minster in 1809.'

Funny Punny Names

Many visitors enjoy reading the names of people on the memorials in the Cathedral. Do you know what a pun is? Sometimes puns are used in a coat of arms. Some families have included their coat of arms on their memorials.

'I am Isabella **Todd**, wife of John Elliot who died in 1834. Three fox heads on our monument make a pun on my name tod, which is another word for fox. When my husband went away without me I was left on my tod (alone).'

The **Bowman** memorial is in the South nave aisle, can

HE

you find it?

Can you spot the three bows and arrows?

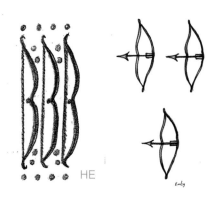 

'My surname is **Bayne** which means bone. Crossed bones are on our family monument. When my husband, Mr Bayne, was cross with me he said, "Hellen, sometimes you are the bane (poison or ruin) of my life." I called him a Bonehead! Then we sang "Them bones, them bones, them dry bones, now hear the word of the Lord" and it made us smile!'

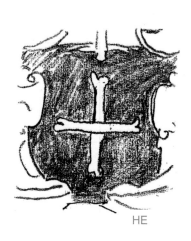 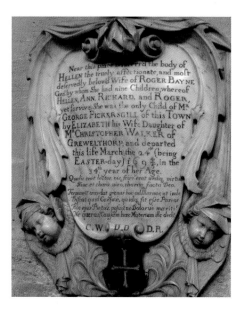

[Helen Entwisle]

Activities

Paint Brush – Fox's Brush

Do you remember Mr and Mrs Tod (which means fox)? Look at the picture of a fox. Can you copy it? Would you use a paint brush or a fox's brush to colour it?! (A fox's tail is called a brush.)

Hatched Line

Do you also remember the Badcock family whose monument shows three cockerels? Look at the picture of the cockerel below. Why not draw one of your own. Short lines sketched close to each other are called hatched lines. Hens also hatch eggs. If there are a lot of eggs does this make a hatched line?!

Look for the symbols in or around the Cathedral:
An **urn** with a flame rising out of it is a sign of new life. Urns which are empty stand for end of life. The urn with a drape around it could be a sign of comfort, like someone putting their arms around you. Or it could be like the curtain closing at the end of a stage play.
How many urns on memorials can you spot in the Cathedral?

Serpent (see Weddell Memorial)
Usually a snake stands for evil but the serpent on the Weddell monument

forms a complete circle with its mouth clinging onto its own tail. This is a symbol of eternal life. Can you find the Weddell memorial and the serpent?

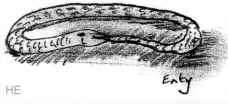

HE

Skull (see Anna Hutchinson memorial)
Not surprisingly a skull symbolises death. Can you find the skull on Anna Hutchinson's memorial? It is carved in alabaster and feels cold and smooth to the touch. This memorial is the North Nave Aisle near the Chapel of Justice and Peace.

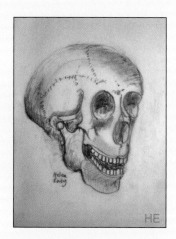

HE

Snowdrop (Henry Strickland Memorial)
Flowers can stand for beauty, peace, youth, old age, life, perfection. On the Strickland Memorial the stem of one of the snowdrops is broken. This is in memory of a child who did not live very long.

HE

Spot the Differences

There are 8 differences between the two pictures of The Hand. Can you find them?

Check your answers here

[Helen Entwisle]

129

Chapter 10

1836 – The Year of Change

Ripon Minster becomes a Cathedral

836 was a year of great change. A new *diocese* of Ripon was created, with a Bishop appointed to control it, and Ripon Minster was made into the Cathedral Church of St Peter and St Wilfrid. This was the first new cathedral in England for three hundred years!

Ripon Minster in 1809, detail from Buckler's etching

This affected the town as well and Ripon consequently became a city. The definition of a city is a large town or any UK town with a cathedral. Ripon had grown in population during the **Industrial Revolution** and become a centre for the local wool trade and manufacturing industries.

The Bishop's Throne

The word **Cathedral** comes from the Latin word 'cathedra' which means 'the throne of a bishop'. The bishops' throne, which in Ripon is quite modest, is found in the choir and has some interesting carvings on it.

Photo: Dean Keith

The Elephant

On the back of the elephant is a castle containing eleven men. These may represent the disciples of Jesus, with Judas, the disciple who betrayed Jesus, held in the elephant's trunk!

Left: carving on the end of the Bishop's throne

Right: The elephant and the castle

The First Bishop of Ripon

Dr Charles Thomas Longley was appointed as the first Bishop of Ripon and was enthroned in the Cathedral on Friday 11th November 1836. He was educated at Christchurch, Oxford (where he gained a first class degree in Classics) and became a tutor at his college and a university examiner, before serving as Headmaster of Harrow School until he was made Bishop of Ripon.

Bishop Longley

A new palace was built for the Bishop, who was married with three sons and three daughters. He served as Bishop of Ripon for twenty years before becoming Bishop of Durham then Archbishop of York. He was made Archbishop of Canterbury in 1862. The Archbishop is the chief bishop and leader of the Church of England and the head of the worldwide Anglican Communion. Charles Longley was the 92nd Archbishop of Canterbury and held the post until his death in 1868. Robert Bickersteth was appointed to replace Longley as Bishop of Ripon in 1857.

The new Bishop's Palace

The Current Bishop of Ripon and Leeds

Bishop John was made Lord Bishop in 2006, when he entered the House of Lords.

Rt Revd John Packer

The Dean and Chapter

The dean is the name given to the senior priest in charge of the day to day running of the Cathedral. The *Chapter* is the body responsible for administering the Cathedral and includes within its number the residentiary canons. These canons are the priests of the Cathedral and live in houses near to the Cathedral. They are responsible for the daily work of the Cathedral, including the ministry of welcome and education. The canon precentor has particular responsibility for the Cathedral music and worship.

The Diocese of Ripon

A diocese is the name for a part of the country under the pastoral care of a bishop of the Church of England. The diocesan arms can be found on the back of the bishop's throne.

Heraldic symbols of the shield

The symbols on a shield or crest often stand for something:

- the **mitre** is the traditional hat worn by a bishop.
- the **crossed keys** are the symbol for St. Peter who is considered to be the gatekeeper of heaven.

Interestingly 'The Crossed Keys', 'The Mitre' and 'The Lamb and Flag' are also the names of local pubs!

[Louise Watson]

The Diocese of Ripon and Leeds

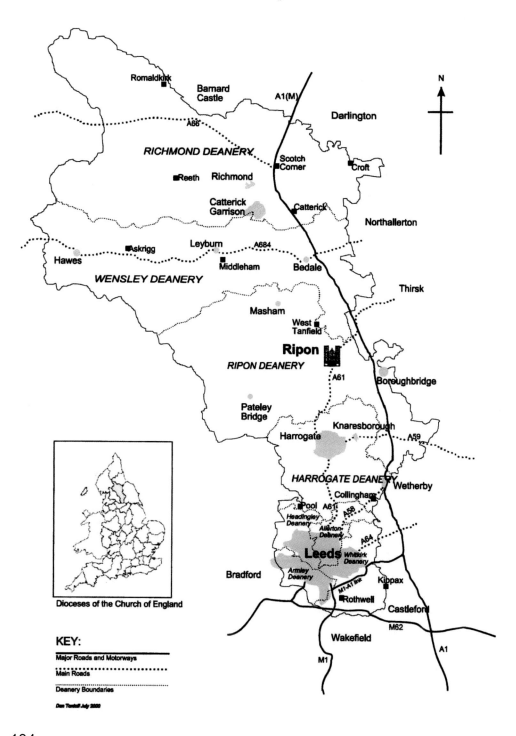

Dioceses of the Church of England

KEY:

Major Roads and Motorways

Main Roads

Deanery Boundaries

Dan Tunstall July 2020

Activities

Bishops of the Past

Can you find a list of all the Bishops of Ripon in the Cathedral?

(Hint: it is near the west end)

A day in the life of the Cathedral

What happens during the day in the Cathedral? When do services take place? Look at the notice boards and leaflets. Is there anything special happening in the Cathedral today?

Design a Crozier

The bishop's staff of office is called a crozier. It is based on a shepherd's crook. As the shepherd looks after his flock, the bishop looks after his people.

A bishop also has a mitre and a cope. Design a set for yourself, keeping in mind that the four colours of the church calendar are red, green, gold and purple.

LT

LT

[Louise Watson]

135

Chapter 11

The House of Bones

Josh and Tilly dug deep into the chest; Josh pulled out what appeared to be a bone, a human bone! Tilly gasped with fright – 'oh no,' she thought, I have a bad feeling about this, but before she could say anything to Josh, the air had become misty and she felt as though they were spinning through space again.

They landed with a bump on the hard, cold floor of Ripon Cathedral. They both recognised it immediately and felt relieved. When the mist cleared, they saw that the Cathedral definitely didn't look the way it should. There was work going on everywhere, the walls of the wonderful west front looked as if they could come crashing down at any minute and they could see sky through the roof.

'What's going on?' Tilly asked.

'How should I know?' said Josh, 'let's find someone and ask.' Just then a man with a set of keys passed by followed closely by a couple dressed in what appeared to be Victorian costumes. Josh and Tilly had just finished studying the Victorians at school so they recognised the style at once. Josh called to the man who looked like his job was to look after the Cathedral, but he appeared not to hear or see them; it was as though they were invisible. They jumped up and followed the little group.

They arrived at a massive door, which the sexton proceeded to unlock, but before he would let the Victorian couple pass he held out his hand and they dropped a large shiny coin into it. He quickly pocketed the coin before slowly pushing open the heavy door to reveal the ghastly contents of the room.

The colour drained from Josh's face and Tilly stifled a scream. Neither of them could believe what was in front of them. Bones, bones and more bones – bones of all shapes and sizes, from tiny skulls, which could only have belonged to babies to great big bones of fully grown men. The bones were all stacked neatly, every skull had a set of arms and legs stacked with them, but they were all muddled like they belonged to different bodies.

Tilly looked green as though she was going to throw up, but the elegantly dressed Victorian couple were having a lovely time. They were completely fascinated by the bones and stopped occasionally to stroke this skull or that. In fact when the twins looked closely they could see that some of the skulls were quite shiny from being touched by visitors.

They listened as the sexton explained proudly that the bones had once been scattered all around the undercroft, but he had stacked them all up so that every skull had some arms and legs. The stacks must have reached two metres high and the walls couldn't be seen. Josh guessed that there must have been the remains of around 600 bodies down there.

All these heads with mismatched arms and legs, lying in the dank air of the dimly lit undercroft made both twins feel queasy and in need of some air.

Just as Tilly looked as though she could faint there was a sudden whooshing sound and they found them selves sitting back where they had started - in front of the chest.

'What was all that about?' gasped Tilly. She had started to get a little colour back, but was still a bit shaky.

'I think we just saw the 'bone house' said Josh.

'What's that?' replied Tilly.

'I'm not sure,' said Josh, 'but I've seen something about it on a memorial in the Cathedral grave yard'.

'Lets go and find it,' said Tilly.

The twins raced round to the Cathedral graveyard and found a plaque in the graveyard wall, which read:

UNDER THIS STONE IS A PIT 12 FEET DEEP. THE EXTENT OF WHICH IS MARKED OUT BY BOUNDARY STONES. A PORTION OF THE BONES THAT WERE IN A CRYPT, UNDER THE SOUTH EASTERN PART OF THE CATHEDRAL WERE BURIED MAY 1865.

And now for the facts ...

Victoria Rules!

Queen Victoria came to the throne in 1837 when she was only eighteen years old. She reigned for 64 years, which is longer than any other monarch in British history.

The Victorian age was very exciting as things were changing quickly. It was a period of industrial, cultural, political, scientific, and military progress within the United Kingdom and new possibilities were opening up for everyone.

Queen Victoria never visited Ripon on an official engagement, but on 7th Sept 1858 the Royal train stopped at Ripon station on its way to Edinburgh and the Queen accepted an address of welcome and spent a short time taking a royal "walkabout".

I think this may have upset our neighbours in Harrogate as they were expecting her to stop there, but instead the train sped through the station and all the crowds saw was a brief glimpse of the Queen who appeared to be asleep at the time!

Gilbert's Glorious Rebuild

Religion was very important to the Victorians and Parliament spent a third of its time talking about religious matters. Most people in a town went to a church service on Sunday and followed strict rules of behaviour. In Ripon in 1891, 1400 people would regularly attend church each Sunday.

For the first time since the English Reformation, which began in 1534 during the reign of Henry VIII, new churches were built and medieval ones restored.

In the mid 1800s Ripon Cathedral was once again in a very poor state, the West Front towers were in danger of collapse and the roofs were so full of holes that rain poured in on to the congregation below.

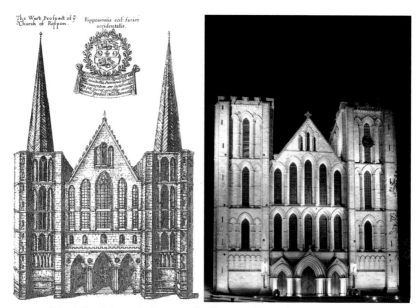

The West front before and after the Victorian restoration

In 1861 a public appeal was begun for donations to restore the Cathedral and work began in 1866. The architect, Sir Gilbert Scott, who was a famous restorer of medieval buildings, planned the work. It took five years to complete and it cost about £40,000, which would be about £2.5 million pounds today!

One of the biggest parts of the renovation was to save the West Front towers from falling down. In the 12th century the West Front had been built on very shallow foundations and the digging of tombs inside the Cathedral had made them even shakier. The walls had moved so much that great big cracks had appeared and it was very dangerous for the workmen as the walls could come crashing in at any time. To make the West Front safe and strong again, the workmen had to dig down nearly 4 metres to strengthen the foundations of the building.

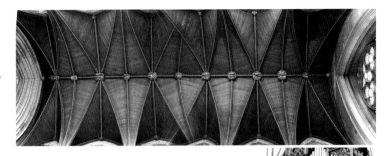

Right: ceiling in the choir, restored in the 1880s under the guidance of Sir George Gilbert Scott

Below: some of the restored canopies

The restorers also replaced the roof in the choir and restored the 15th century ceilings in the transepts.

Another big job was to restore the beautiful carved canopies and misericords in the choir stalls, which had been damaged when the central spire fell in 1660. If you look at the canopies in the choir you can just see a slight change in the colour of the wood, this shows where the original canopies end and the restoration work begins.

At the end of the massive restoration project in 1871 the Cathedral looked very much like it does today. There was a special service to celebrate the renovation where the Dean of York Minster spoke and afterwards there was a lunch at the town hall, which was attended by all the important people of Ripon and those who had donated big sums of money towards the renovation. It must have been a very exciting day for the people of Ripon.

Wonderful Windows Return to Ripon

During the Reformation stained glass windows were smashed or taken out of churches as they were seen as too fancy and the skilled art of making stained glass, which had been passed down over generations, was almost forgotten. However, the Victorians loved medieval architecture and stained glass became popular again. Most of the beautiful windows in Ripon Cathedral are from the Victorian Era.

These windows were very expensive to make and were paid for by wealthy local families who wanted to have a window in the Cathedral as a memorial to a member of their family or to show that they were people of high morals who wanted to be remembered for their good deeds.

Murder & the Greek Bandits

A famous window in the Cathedral is the one dedicated to Frederick Vyner; it can be seen in the North choir aisle. This window recalls the tragic death of young Frederick who was captured and murdered by Greek Terrorists whilst taking a holiday in Athens in 1870.

Fredrick was 23 and during his holiday from University, he visited Marathon near Athens with a party of well-to-do British visitors. The party took lots of precautions to ensure their safety on the trip, but even so they were ambushed and taken as hostages.

A large ransom of £32,000, which would be about £2 million today was demanded for their safe release. The Greek Government & The British Government were involved in the negotiations to free the prisoners, but the

Above: memorial window to the murdered Frederick Grantham Vyner

Left: the bottom-right panel from the same window, showing the intricate craftsmanship involved in glass staining and painting, cutting and insertion in a lead framework

142

talks were handled badly. In the end soldiers were sent to free the hostages, but during the shoot out the prisoners were executed by the bandits and half of the bandit gang was allowed to escape.

Frederick needn't have lost his life, as during his kidnap ordeal the gang had agreed to free him to act as a messenger for them, but Frederick heroically let another hostage go free in his place.

The Greeks were very embarrassed by their failure to rescue the innocent men and for a time relations between the Greek and the British governments were badly affected. As compensation for the tragedy the Greek government paid the Vyner family a big sum of money. The money was used by his grieving family for the beautiful window in the Cathedral and also to build two churches near Ripon to Fredrick's memory. The churches are the Church of Christ the Consoler at Skelton-on-Ure and the other is the Church of St Mary at Studley.

Endless Empire

The British Empire was at its greatest during Victorian times and at the end of 19th century the British Empire covered a fifth of the world and there were 400 million people in it. A big empire meant that there was an increase in trade with trading ships being sent all over the world carrying goods to and from distant places.

Ripon played its part in sending men to far off lands in the Empire, either to fight, to work in the government, to trade or to explore.

In the Cathedral you can see memorials to people who lost their life helping to build the Empire and they also tell stories of how hard it was for some of them.

Two memorials that are very sad are those for two brothers, the Waddiloves, who were grandsons of The Very Revd, R. D. Waddilove who had once been a dean of the Cathedral. One brother was a soldier and the other was a sailor. They both died overseas and their bodies

The Waddilove brothers, Lt. Francis and Lt. Robert were descended from a former Dean in Ripon Cathedral. Both died in serving their country overseas. Their memorials are in the north transept.

never came home to Ripon, but the memorials mean we can remember them here.

The sailor, Robert Waddilove, died in 1844 on his ship in the South Pacific and he was buried at sea. He was only 25 years old when he died, but he had served in the Royal Navy since the age of twelve!

His brother Francis Waddilove died in India in 1849. Like his brother he was only 25 years old. The memorial tells how his regiment were ordered to march for over 250 miles in heat that was over 100F (nearly 39C). Frances Waddilove completed the march, although many others died of the unbearable heat. However, it had made him terribly ill and he died a few days later. Francis had also served the Empire in Ireland and in Canada. His family must have been terribly upset and angry to have lost their brave son so needlessly.

Another important figure from Ripon who played a big part in the Empire was the 1st Marquess of Ripon – George Frederick Robinson. He was the owner of Fountains Abbey and was the Viceroy of India between 1880 and 1885. This was a very important position; it meant that he was the Queen's official representative in India, ruling it on her behalf.

The Marquess of Ripon has a heraldic window in the Cathedral and there is a big statue of him in Spa Gardens.

Was Ripon Alice's Wonderland?

In early Victorian times it was thought that children should only read for education, that books should be serious and all about religious teachings and right and wrong. Lewis Carroll (whose real name was Charles Dodgson) changed this with his Alice Stories, which led the way for other authors to write stories that children would enjoy and laugh over.

It is often said that Ripon and Ripon Cathedral provided some of the inspiration for the Alice Stories. How much of that is true we really don't know, but Ripon did play a part in Lewis's life.

Lewis's father was a Canon at Ripon Cathedral and for 13 weeks of each year Lewis lived in The Old Hall, which is the house at the bottom of the steps on the South side of the Cathedral.

He visited the Cathedral often and will have spent time looking at the beautiful carvings of fabulous fantasy creatures carved on the misericord seats. It is believed that the carving of a rabbit being chased down a hole by a griffin may have inspired the part in his story where Alice followed the

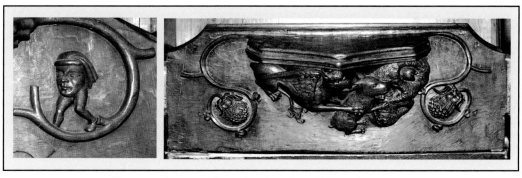

Two carvings on the misericords in Ripon Cathedral

Left:: a blemya   Right: the griffin chasing rabbits

white rabbit down the hole. Also the carving of the blemya (a medieval mythical creature), which is a monster with his head on top of his legs, looks very like the drawing of Alice after she ate a piece of mushroom and shrank.

There are many other reasons why people believe that Ripon influenced the Alice stories. The original drawing of Alice was taken from a photograph of Mary Babcock, the daughter of the Head Master of the Ripon College. Also, Ripon is troubled with something called gypsum subsidence, where the rocks under the land dissolve away and suddenly collapse to leave a big deep tunnel. Lewis may have seen these tunnels suddenly appear and he may have been inspired by them to write about Alice dropping "down, down, down, to land bump, bump, bump".

We will never know for sure how much Lewis was inspired by Ripon and the Cathedral, but when Scott was completing his restoration of the Cathedral's South transept ceiling he included a Queen of Hearts and a grinning Cheshire Cat, to remember Lewis's link with Ripon Cathedral.

It's all Black!

In 1861 Queen Victoria's husband Albert died at the age of 42. Queen Victoria loved her husband very much and was devastated by his death. She went into a period of mourning, which lasted for the rest of her life.

Following her example it became normal for Victorian families to go to a lot of trouble to remember their dead and the rules about it all got quite complicated. Books were written to give instructions on what was the right thing to do when a relative or friend died.

Victorians wore mourning clothes, which were black, and they had to wear them for different lengths of time depending on how close they were to the dead person. If he was your husband you were expected to wear mourning clothes for two years.

To the Victorians a funeral became the last big important event in a person's life. It was also a chance for the dead and their families to show off how important they were and how much money they had. Therefore Victorian funerals became big business, with families being encouraged to have very expensive funerals and to put up fancy monuments on graves and memorials in churches.

Tragedy on the Train

HE

A memorial that you can look for in Ripon Cathedral is the one to Fanny Whitaker. Fanny's story is a tragic one, because Fanny was only 29 when she died and her death was caused by a railway accident.

Rail transport had become very popular for passengers during the Victorian era and was changing the way people lived. For the first time it became easy for working class people to travel further than ten miles in a day and day trips to new places were within the reach of most people.

On the day in question, Fanny Whitaker was travelling from Harrogate to York with some friends. She was in a first class compartment, which was right for a well brought up young lady of the time. At Green Hammerton something went wrong with the points on the track and the carriage that Fanny was travelling in was violently overturned, throwing Fanny out of the window. The carriage then seemed to stand back up before it fell over again on to where Fanny was lying. Fanny was still alive, but she died the following day of her dreadful injuries.

When Fanny's body was taken through Ripon for burial in Kirby Malzeard the minute bell of the Cathedral tolled and shops were closed out of respect for Fanny and her family.

An Amazing Age Draws to an End

The Victorian era came to an end on 22 January 1901 when Queen Victoria died. She had reigned for 63 years, 7 months and 2 days; the longest of any British Monarch before or since and the longest reigning female monarch of all time.

After spending most of her years after the death of Prince Albert wearing

black, Queen Victoria was buried wearing a white dress and her wedding veil. The horses carrying her coffin were white and all funeral decorations around the city of London were either white or purple.

Queen Victoria's funeral was also one of the first major royal events to be captured by the new film industry with several new film companies releasing flickering footage of the funeral procession.

[Carolyn Sands]

The clock tower on North Street was erected to mark 50 years of Queen Victoria's reign

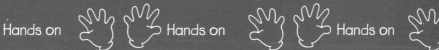
Activities

In the footsteps of Lewis Carroll ...

… here are two projects for you

1. Have a look at the fantasy animals carved on the misericords in the choir of the Cathedral and design your own fictional character based on one of them. Think of a name that would suit the character. You could even write a story or poem about your character.

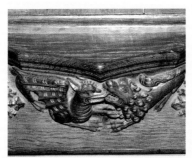

2. Find the **Cheshire Cat** and the **Queen of Hearts** in the South transept. (You will have to look up, up, up)

[Carolyn Sands]

149

A Heart of Gold

A Victorian tale by pupils at

St Wilfrid's RC Primary School, year 6

This painting served as inspiration for 'A Heart of Gold'

St Martin-in-the-Fields, 1888

William Logsdail

© Tate, London 2010

Olivia Violet Taylor was nowhere near as posh as her name would suggest. Instead she was a poor flower girl, earning money to help her family pay the rent on the little terraced house on Ure Bank Top, near to Ripon Railway Station, where her Dad worked the signals for the trains to pass. Although life was tough for her, Olivia was a happy girl, with a loving family and enough food to eat, though barely enough sometimes.

In winter, as she tramped the cold, cobbled streets of Ripon, selling whatever flowers and foliage she could find in the hedge rows and woods to brighten the big parlours of rich people passing by, she dreamed that one day she would be like them. She would live in a grand house, like those in the Crescent, whose windows she glimpsed through at Christmas time as she tried to sell the holly twigs, laden with bright red berries whose leaves had prickled and scratched at her thin little hands. She would marry a rich man and have dresses made of silk and shiny black buttoned boots for her neat little feet. She would have servants to clean and to cook for her and a personal maid to care for her every need – one day.

In summer, as she wandered in the sunny Spring Bank Meadows, amongst the myriad of colourful wild flowers – cowslips and willow herbs, buttercups and cornflowers, she dreamt of having her very own garden with well kept camomile lawns and a rose garden brimming with red and white roses that scented the warm air. She would walk in the shade of the apple trees, carrying her parasol so that the sun would not dazzle her ocean blue eyes. A sailor, home from a sea voyage, had teased her with this when he bought a tiny posy from her once in the market place. She remembered it on dreaming days and it made her feel special. But Olivia knew that this was not reality, the only time SHE got to have beautiful flowers around her was when she was selling them from her pitch in front of the town hall or by the tall obelisk in the market place.

As Olivia trudged her way towards the peaceful churchyard to put the remaining flowers from today on her brother Thomas' simple grave, she felt a surge of sadness as she remembered how he had been trampled on by a horse and carriage passing too quickly through the centre of the town. She had heard his cry as the carriage rolled over him. She would never forget him- he had been strong and the family relied on him to earn his living. His hair, and his face, had been as black as the coal he stoked into the steam trains.

But now it was Meg, the oldest of her brothers and sisters, whom she looked up to. Meg was sixteen and had long silky blonde hair, as fair as her brother's had been dark. Olivia would have swapped her own tangle of waves for Meg's silky tresses any day. Meg looked after the family while mother was doing all her many jobs. She was sensible and kind but often suffered with her chest, wheezing and coughing so much sometimes that Olivia would worry. Doctors' bills were expensive and they had no money to spare. Then there were the twins, William and George. They were only one year younger than Olivia and were "like chalk and cheese", Ma would say. Susannah, a bit of a busy body, was the second youngest, and then there was little Lily. Olivia knew that in a family you shouldn't have favourites, but if she was allowed, Lily would have been her favourite.

Olivia laid her flowers by the simple cross and turned towards home. She worried about what her Pa would say when he saw the little she had earned that day. She had hoped that rich, kind Lady Christina would have given her a tip today, but alas she had not appeared and Olivia went home the poorer for it.

As she approached the front door of her house Olivia heard a booming voice, so loud she shuddered, recognising it as the angry voice of the landlord, Lord Eduardo Carlisle. It was not the first time she had heard it and she knew that trouble would surely follow. Tentatively she opened the door and slipped into the tiny front room. His voice seemed to fill the whole of the house and then by contrast, she heard her mother's gentle, reasoned tones. "Just wait till Olivia returns home" she was saying, "then we'll have enough to pay, with the money she has earned today."

Olivia felt faint as she gingerly entered the room. Her mother's smiley face turned grim as Olivia slowly opened her hand to reveal the very little she had earned that day. "Right, you have had your chance!" roared Lord Eduardo, "I have no more time and no more money to waste - and I have no pity for the miserable poor who can't pay their rent. Your job is lost to you now Mr Taylor. I shall see to that! It's the workhouse for you and your family."

And before they could protest they were roughly turned out by the landlord and his two mean-faced ruffians and cast onto the street. Olivia noticed a single tear roll down her mother's face as they were marched off to the Workhouse. "Hold your heads up high and keep close to me," Ma whispered.

Although the workhouse was inevitable now, Ma and Pa were proud and dignified... We may be poor but we're not stupid; we'll find a way out of this," said Pa and he set his jaw tight against all that was to follow.

But Olivia was determined. The workhouse was the last place she would go. She wriggled free of the landlord's tight grasp and darted into a dark alleyway on the brim of the hill. She waited in the darkness and after a while peered out nervously.

"What now?" she wondered. Slowly an idea came into Olivia's head. She would creep into the small barn on the roadside at "Apple Tree Farm". Then tomorrow she would work out something. She would find a way to help her family and herself. There must be a way.

Olivia woke with a start. She saw what she thought was a scarecrow staring down at her –a kind sort of scarecrow that turned out to be a boy with a big friendly grin and spiky, yellow hair – just like corn in a field. His tall skinny figure was leaning over her and in his outstretched hand was a plate of crusty bread with creamy, smooth butter, which he placed beside her as he knelt down.

"Don't worry, you don't need to be frightened of me," he said in a chirpy manner.

"What's your name?" said Olivia, nervous at being discovered so quickly.

"Charlie Miller, at your service, ma'am" he said and grinned cheekily, his blue eyes, as bright as cornflowers, were twinkling. Olivia instantly knew they would be friends.

"Olivia Taylor at yours!" she said brightly, in return.

"No need to be scared of me," said Charlie Miller. "I often find strangers sleeping in here. Must need to, I reckon, so I don't go asking questions. What you don't know you can't tell. Know what I mean? Makes life int'resting," he said mischievously. Olivia gobbled her breakfast and then brushed herself down. She was very dusty from lying in the straw all night.

"Is this your barn then Charlie?" asked Olivia.

"Ay!" he said," Well it's my grandad's. I live with him 'ere. My Ma and Pa are dead and gone to heaven you see... I scare the birds away – it's boring and lonely and it can be very cold on wet days, but it 'elps me grandad's corn to grow – for where would we be if that failed us - the workhouse, no doubt!"

Olivia smiled ruefully at that and began to tell Charlie her story too.

"Well I'd better be getting on. We've all got work to do." said Charlie. "You might like these" he said, depositing a basket of apples at her feet. "I'll see you later –that's if you decide to stay." And with that Charlie disappeared through the barn door.

"Wait!" cried Olivia, but when she looked outside he was nowhere to be seen. She sighed a deep sigh and walked towards the meadows where she usually gathered her flowers. In one of the fields she found some lovely red poppies and harebells, and in a tiny corner near the wooden fence she discovered a little patch of juicy green, gooseberries and added them to the basket of apples which Charlie had given her along with a few of the nicest poppies and began to make her way towards the market place. On her way she noticed a happy family walking hand in hand together –two children out for a stroll with their parents. She thought of her own family, now split up and separate.

As she entered the little florist's shop, where she sometimes bought violets for someone's special request, her sadness made her forget that she had no money to buy anything at all, today.

"Hello, my little flower girl" said the old gentleman behind the counter. "Are you here to buy your violets again?

"Yes please, just a bundle." she said politely.

"Right, little lady. That will be a halfpenny, if you please," smiled the old man.

Searching in her pockets Olivia realised she had nothing. She was near to tears with embarrassment and feeling foolish, whispered, "I have no money today, I forgot. I'm so sorry".

The old man, knowing how hard Olivia worked to help her family, felt sorry for the girl.

"Not to worry my dear," he said kindly, "today, my violets are free – but only to you," and he bowed graciously as he handed her the tiny, fragrant bunch. Olivia was overwhelmed. She was reminded that in this harsh world there were still good and generous –hearted people.

"Thank you, you are most kind" she said, fighting back her tears. As she disappeared from the shop back into the street she felt a new hope in her own heart that things might, just might, get better.

It was a busy Thursday afternoon and trading was good at the market. The market traders were shouting to attract customers to their colourful stalls. There were pears and plums from the orchards nearby, milk in tall churns from the farm dairies and cheese churned as far away as Wensleydale, fish and fresh crabs all the way from Redcar, fleeces ready to be spun and expensive cloths from the newest factories in Bradford. Behind her Olivia could smell the baked potatoes and the hot meat pies. She could hear the voices of the policemen as they chased young pick pockets along the streets and ginnels and the horses' hooves trotting on the cobbled streets as carriages sailed by. Olivia took up her stance by the obelisk and found that even for her, business was good today. It wasn't long before a familiar and very welcome figure came into her sights through the busy crowds.

"Lady Christina!" Olivia shouted out, without thinking, as a slender figure clad from head to toe in the finest red satin turned and smiled warmly at her.

"How are you today, my dear little flower girl" she asked, the corners of her lips turning up a little, the happiness at seeing the girl clear on her face.

"Fine Madam, thank you", said Olivia, bobbing demurely. "I have some of your favourite flowers today, if you would like them, and some lovely summer fruits to tempt you, too."

"Wonderful," laughed the fine lady, a glint in her soft, hazel brown eyes. I'll have five of your beautiful violets as a bunch, and an apple and some gooseberries too."

"That will be five half pennies please" said Olivia, as she was handed five whole pennies. "Thank you kindly, generous Ma'am," whispered Olivia, suppressing her joy at being favoured once more by Lady Christina's charity.

"No, no. It is I who must thank you, my dear, for these lovely fresh flowers. Good bye, my little Olivia."

Charlie jumped off the hay bale he had been standing on to try and see if Olivia was coming. As she approached the gate he ran out to greet her.

"There you are at last," he cried, pleased to see her again. "Come on before my Grandpa comes in from the fields" he whispered excitedly.

Over the next few days Charlie and Olivia's friendship grew. Charlie would have bread and cheese waiting for her when she returned from town, sometimes bread and strawberry jam and a large cup filled with home-made lemonade or fresh cool milk. She would only realise how hungry she had grown when she began to eat.

Then they would talk and Charlie learned more about Olivia, her interests and her family problems. Olivia would tell Charlie of the people she met and he loved to hear about Lady Christina. One night Charlie seemed different, more excited than usual.

"I have something to show you!" he was in very high spirits, "it's the answer to all your problems," and with that he produced from his pocket a beautiful gold heart - shaped locket that shimmered and shone. "It's made of the finest gold!" he said and bit hard on it.

"Don't damage it!" called out Olivia in alarm.

"That's just to test its worth," he said with a grin.

"It's extraordinary! So beautiful. Where did you get it, Charlie? You didn't steal it did you?" she said, suddenly alarmed.

Charlie was hurt that she could think such a thing, but she apologised and he was quick to forgive her.

"Today, I came to the marketplace to find you. I was just about to cross over, close to the Unicorn Inn, where the carriages stop, when I noticed something shining on the cobbles there. It was this locket and chain. I looked around but no-one was watching, so I pocketed it quickly and then ran all the way back home. I've been waiting to show you," his face was a picture.

Olivia took the locket into her hands; somehow it looked familiar and Olivia tried hard to think where she had seen it before. Noticing a tiny catch on the side, Olivia gently opened the locket only to find herself looking at a portrait of a young woman remarkably like Lady Christina! On the other side was the portrait of an older lady, but with the same rosy cheeks, the same slender neck and the same pretty smile. Olivia realised that it was indeed Lady Christina and her mother, perhaps. She must have lost it today as she got out of the carriage that brought her into town.

Suddenly Olivia was on her feet and racing along the country lane.

"Olivia, come back!" cried Charlie in dismay. "Why are you running away from me? Don't you like the locket?"

Olivia slowed down and waited.

"I thought you would be pleased" Charlie's voice was filled with disappointment. "I thought if I gave it to you it would pay your rent, free your family from the workhouse ---I thought ---"

Olivia interrupted him. "I AM happy Charlie, I'm sorry if I seem ungrateful. But I know who this locket belongs to. I have seen Lady

Christina wearing it. She's been so kind to me. Now we can repay her."

"But can't we just keep it?" Charlie pleaded. "After all - finders' keepers, they say."

"I can't do that Charlie" said Olivia gently, "wouldn't you want something precious returned to you?"

"I suppose so," Charlie reluctantly agreed.

Together they made their way down towards town. It was getting dark and the gas lamps were beginning to be lit. Olivia knew of the Crescent but had never ventured near. Nervously Olivia and Charlie tiptoed towards the grand circle of houses. In the window of one Olivia saw the unmistakeable figure of Lady Christina. She was wearing the same red dress that Olivia had so admired that day. Timidly they moved towards the big front door. Its brass knocker glinted golden in the lamplight. Olivia raised her arm to knock, when suddenly the door was flung open and Olivia and Charlie were shooed harshly away. "We want no beggars around here; up to no good I'll be bound!" came the booming voice of a man servant. Olivia tried to protest, Charlie tried to explain.

All of a sudden Lady Christina appeared and was shocked to see her little flower girl before her. Her hand was stroking her bare neck even as she spoke to them, as if reaching for the lost locket. Olivia stretched out her hand and thrust the locket at Lady Christina.

"I think this belongs to you, Ma'am," she stuttered. "I have seen you wearing it, I'm sure." Lady Christina gasped, her eyes widening with joy.

"My locket, my most precious locket" she cried "But how ---?" Of course she listened to all they had to say and was overwhelmed with joy at receiving her most precious piece of jewellery once more. "I can't tell you just how much this means to me" she told them. "I must find a way---" "and her voice trailed off. They were given gingerbread biscuits and lemonade before setting back on their way to the farm. Lady Christina watched and waved as her young friends departed.

"Oh well," said Charlie, it seems our troubles are not over after all.

"We'll never get a better chance than that." And they both fell into silence, not knowing what might happen next.

Next morning Olivia and Charlie shared breakfast together once more. They talked about Christina and yesterday's adventure. She knew Charlie had spirit and loved adventures, but was glad he had done the right thing and told him so. Charlie seemed to grow three inches in the light of Olivia's praise.

Olivia was sure that there had been sadness in Lady Christina's life too and that somehow her life inside the big house was not as wonderful as it seemed. Reuniting her with her mother's portrait hidden inside the golden locket made Olivia feel very proud. It had brought a smile to Lady Christina's face and made her happy.

Suddenly another thought leapt into Olivia's mind. Why could everyone else with their family whilst she could not? She missed them all dreadfully and yearned to see them again. But she had heard such tales of the workhouse! It was not the place for her, she was sure about that. However, she suddenly became determined, and without thinking twice, marched towards the workhouse for the poor and destitute of Ripon.

It was only as she drew near to the large iron gates that Olivia had doubts. Nevertheless, she climbed to the very top and let herself down, landing with a bump on the other side. She approached a nearby window just to see what it was like inside. That was her mistake! Lord Eduardo Carlisle was talking in what seemed a very official manner to a large and rather stern gentleman with a strange triangular shaped hat on his head and an ornate gold decoration on his black cape.

As soon as Olivia put her head above the window sill Lord Eduardo spotted her. She was certainly done for now! She made a run for the gate and started to climb back over it but just as she reached the top she felt a strong clasping hand pulling her back. She landed with a thud at Lord Eduardo's feet and blood spurted out of a cut on her knee. He smiled with a strange pleasure as he recognised her. How she hated this man!

"You little wretch, so you think you can escape me a second time, eh?" he snarled like a mad dog. "You can come into the workhouse with the other rats," he bellowed, his eyes narrowing into slits.

"That's why I came - to get my family back!" Olivia retorted bravely.

"Speaking without permission! No gruel tonight! You are going to have a hard time here missy!" he smiled his horrible smile once more.

Lord Eduardo dragged Olivia towards the door of the workhouse and pulled her inside. Nothing seemed very welcoming. There were stone walls and sharp granite floors. She was marched into a room filled with wooden beds. The room was empty. Lord Eduardo left and locked the door behind him. Nothing mattered to Olivia now. She was in the workhouse to stay! She lay on a bed exhausted and fell into a deep and troubled sleep.

Olivia was woken by a harsh clanging bell and someone lightly touching her arm. She opened her eyes and to her amazement saw the face of Meg smiling down at her. "Meg!" yelled Olivia. They hugged one another tightly.

"Let's go down for breakfast before Miss Grimmer sees us. She'll give you a slap and a half, if you break any rules," warned Meg. Glad to be together once more the girls, led by Meg almost ran towards the big room filled with two long tables where everyone sat silently, waiting for a meagre bowl of gruel to see them through the day.

"Meg and Olivia Taylor, no gruel today! You were seen running in the corridor," a grim voice from the fat faced woman in charge screeched out at them. She too wore a mean smile beneath her bulging cheeks.

"Very well," Miss Grimmer, Ma'am" replied Meg, nudging Olivia to do the same. Olivia obliged but with little enthusiasm. "Yes, Miss Grimmer" (another nudge from Meg.) "Ma'am" and they sat back down at the table. Then suddenly who should enter the room but little Lily.

"Olivia!" she squealed with delight. "Lily!" Olivia shouted with equal delight.

"No gruel today, Lily Taylor" again the voice boomed out at them. "To work everyone - except the Taylor brats. You're for the coal bunker all day. That will teach you some manners!"

After a miserable few days Olivia's fingers grew sore with blisters from weaving rag strips into rugs. She moaned a little with the pain. Just then the door creaked open.

"Another poor family for the workhouse," she thought, sympathetically.

She looked up to see who it might be.

"M' – M' – M'Lady", Olivia stuttered. "Wh-What are you doing here? YOU can't possibly be coming to the workhouse too?"

Lady Christina laughed. "Of course not, my dear child! Quite the opposite, in fact. I'm here to take you OUT of this dreadful place!"

Olivia's eyes opened a fraction wider.

"You can't go home quite straightaway, however, my dear" said Christina, "for I have a small amount of paperwork to do first."

Olivia was a little disappointed, for she couldn't wait to see her Pa and Ma again, but at least she felt a little hope in her heart, at last.

"How can I ever repay you?" she cried.

"By holding your tongue, being silent, and getting on with your work, you rude girl!" the harsh voice of the officer in charge broke in.

Lady Christina glared fiercely at him. "I shall see you again, later, my little flower girl" she spoke kindly smiling at Olivia, and then swept out of the room. A little of Olivia's hope, it has to be said, left with her.

The hours that followed seemed to pass painfully slowly for Olivia. She began to grow eager and found it difficult to sit still. As Lady Christina entered the room once more, Olivia almost jumped out of her seat with excitement. The most joyful sight she had ever seen was there before her. Her family, looking dirty and ragged, but alive and well, were there and filled with joy to be together once more.

"Olivia!" they cried with one voice, and rushed towards her as she raced towards them. It was like a stampede!

"Mother, Father, Meg, William, George --and –and –" she stammered, as the little toddler leaped into her outstretched arms, "Lilly!"

"Olivia, my dear, brave girl! What a time of it you have had all on your own!" her Mother wept, as she hugged Olivia close once more.

After a little while, when the tears had dried Lady Christina peeped out of the room and waved someone forward.

"You can come in now, too" she whispered and from out of the shadowy doorway a slight figure emerged. It was Charlie and he was grinning from ear to ear, whether with embarrassment or pride, it was hard to tell.

"It is Charlie who has saved you from this terrible ordeal, not me" said Lady Christina graciously.

"He is the hero of this tale. For it was he, who was worried when you vanished, Olivia, and he, who came to me for help. I had hoped for a way to repay you both for returning my gold heart locket. Charlie showed me the way, and here we are!"

Olivia gave Charlie an enormous hug. "Thank you Charlie," she said and explained to her puzzled family all that had happened.

The Taylor family grew to love Charlie as if he was one of their own and he and his grandfather were always welcome in their home.
Olivia and Charlie were to spend many happy times together. Their friendship was never to end. Sometimes they were invited to the big house in the Crescent for a roast beef dinner served on shiny white plates and cooked by the newly appointed cook – a certain "Mrs Taylor" And in the centre of the polished table would be a little posy of violets perhaps, or roses, especially gathered for the occasion by Olivia, the little flower girl with the help of course of Charlie, (when he wasn't scaring birds or sheltering travellers in his barn). After all, as Lady Olivia was often heard to remark, she wasn't the only person in this world to possess a "Heart of Gold!"

Chapter 12

The Beefeater

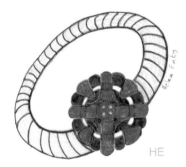

'Do you like this hair bobble?' Tilly asked Josh, as she reached into the chest. She twisted the strap of a large red, white and blue rosette around her pony tail.

Before Josh could answer, the now familiar feeling took them back in time, and the children found themselves in the Cathedral, hidden behind a large, beautiful flower display. Peering out from behind the floral arrangement, they saw that the church was full of people in smart clothes, and most of the ladies were wearing hats.

'How weird, I thought we had gone back in time again, but look at those lines of people standing looking towards the West door – they are wearing modern clothes,' Tilly said.

'Most of them are elderly, and you are right, they do look up to date. But who are those men in the funny red and yellow outfits?' whispered

Josh.

Tilly turned her head to look where her brother pointed and saw men standing to attention in red tunics and tights, with black hats on. They were holding long poles, with spikes on the top. 'Those look like ancient weapons,' she said. 'How can we have past and present at the same time?'

Josh exclaimed, 'They're Beefeaters, Yeomen of the Guard! They must have come from the Tower of London!'

'Sshh!' urged Tilly, realizing that everyone else was standing silently, looking at the door, as if they were expecting something or someone important to come inside. Gradually, they could hear the noise of an excited crowd outside getting louder and louder, until the door opened and some figures stepped inside. Josh and Tilly crept out in front of the flower display, and climbed up onto one of the pews so that they could get a better view of the visitors.

'It's the Queen!' Sure enough, there was Queen Elizabeth II wearing a blue coat and matching hat, with her husband Prince Philip, the Duke of Edinburgh, beside her. The children watched the royal couple walk down the aisle, followed by a procession of smartly dressed companions.

'I wish I was a bodyguard,' said Josh. 'They would teach me karate, and I'd be a great hero.'

Tilly smiled at her brother's fantasy, but did not take her eyes off what was happening. She saw that two brightly dressed Yeomen carrying gold plates heaped up with little money bags were also following the Queen down towards the high altar.

Suddenly, an urgent voice behind the children whispered, 'What are you doing in here? It's Maundy Thursday, the only people the Queen will give Maundy Money to are elderly people who have been specially

164

chosen for doing something good for the community! All the flower girls and other children are supposed to be outside the West front!'

Guiltily, Josh and Tilly jumped down from their vantage point and ran towards the door. Luckily, everyone was looking towards the royal couple, so no-one else noticed them.

Outside, they felt confused to see a huge crowd of people gathered to wait for the Queen to make an appearance. However, before they could decide what to do next, they were told to go and join a small group of children. A tall lady thrust a lovely posy of spring flowers into Tilly's hand, and said,

'Now remember how lucky you are to have been chosen to present the Queen with flowers. You will remember today, Maundy Thursday 1985, for the rest of your life.'

Next she told Josh to go and stand with the waiting crowd. 'Only one pupil from each Ripon primary school will give the posies, everyone else has got to watch from over there.'

Before long a row of yeomen of the Guard marched out of the Cathedral and stood in a semicircle. Tilly followed the other girls and stood in front of them. In a daze, Tilly watched Elizabeth II and the Duke of Edinburgh walk towards them, and copied the curtsey of the other girls as she presented the flowers to the Queen.

Then suddenly the beefeater behind Tilly pulled out her fancy red, white and blue hair bobble, saying, 'That's one of my knee garters. Where on earth did you find it?'

Back once more in the present, kneeling beside the old chest, Tilly said, 'That teacher was right, I will never forget seeing the Queen when she visited Ripon Cathedral in 1985.'

Queen Elizabeth II visits Ripon Cathedral, 1985

HE

And now for the facts ...

In Living Memory

 uring the last hundred years or so, people of all ages have visited the Cathedral for many reasons: baptisms, weddings, funerals, Christmas carol services, tours, school trips, flower shows and concerts. Visitors also sometimes attend church services, light a candle, pray or just enjoy the quiet, spiritual atmosphere of this beautiful building.

This chapter includes quotations taken from a 2009 oral history project about the life of the Cathedral. Is there anyone you could speak to about their memories of services or events in the Cathedral?

A Better Building

During the twentieth century an enormous amount of money was spent on refurbishing the Cathedral. Some of the work is invisible from the ground, such as repairs to the roof. But if you look carefully you can see where some ancient material has been replaced in the last few decades. For example, it is possible to see the work that was done to renew the decaying, fragile limestone around the windows so that it is safe and doesn't fall on anyone below.

Also, work has been done to make it more comfortable for modern congregations. For instance, pipes were fed through a four feet thick stone wall to bring heat from the gas boiler, which was installed to make sure that the nave and choir were warm enough for people used to central heating in their homes. Radiators were even put high above the nave in an attempt to stop all of the hot air from escaping up to the top of the vaulted ceiling.

In 1970 the South choir aisle was converted into the Chapel of the Holy Spirit. The gleaming metal work was designed by Leslie Durbin. It is designed to suggest the flames of Pentecost.

The stone screen West of the choir had probably stood there for 500

years without anyone spending the money to put statues in its arches. The statues of kings and archbishops, with the row of smaller angels above them, were installed in 1947. Twenty years later they were painted and gilded.

The nave furnishing has changed significantly at many times during living memory. For example, the bronze pulpit was erected in 1913. It is decorated with images of Saints. Until the 1930s there was no altar West of the choir stalls. Later, the altar was brought closer to the pulpit, and it now occupies a prominent place in

Top photo: metal screen, Chapel of the Holy Spirit
Centre: stone 'pulpitum' screen between the crossing and the choir   Right: pulpit

the nave.

Nowadays, one of the first things a visitor notices are the new oak chairs, handcrafted locally to replace the oak pews.

Many other improvements have been made during living memory. For example, three new bells were added to the existing ten, and a bell-ringer recalls, "the big bell would be a good six feet in diameter." A musician comments that, "the organ was rebuilt quite significantly over the first half of the twentieth century."

Human and animal bones have been dug up in various parts of the Cathedral, when work has been done. A stonemason remembers 1956, "…we started on the undercroft. The bones from 22 coffins were reburied in the churchyard." In 1997 an archaeological excavation of the crypt uncovered the skeleton of a medieval woman. She had a deformed spine, probably because wealthy women in those days wore a tight belt under their breasts to give them a fashionably small high waist.

Modern Marvels

In 1999, around 100 stitchers, some working in groups, began to make the tapestry cushions and kneelers which make the Cathedral so comfortable and colourful. The cushions, which were designed to mark the Millennium, show scenes from the history of Ripon and represent different local organisations, including the schools.

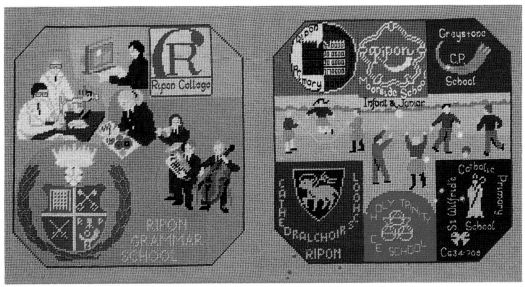

Above: All of Ripon's schools are shown on this Millennium cushion

Below: set of three sculptures of Jesus' life

The three copper statues of Christ were commissioned in 1998. The sculptor was Harold Gosney, who designed them to show Christ with his mother Mary in different stages of his life: as a baby, as a toddler and at his death.

At the end of the twentieth century, the little Cathedral bookshop began to sell modern gifts so it could raise more money to help with the very expensive upkeep of the ancient building. Nowadays it sells all sorts of popular ornaments and jewellery, and even Ripon Jewel beer.

As part of the city's Millennium celebrations in 2000, a time capsule was preserved under the platform holding the Tudor font as a gift to future generations. It contains writings by children, which reflect upon life and worship in the late twentieth century. It will be opened after 100 years, so we can see how much times have changed.

Terrific Technology

Although Ripon Cathedral is well over a thousand years old, modern technology is used in many ways. For example, many religious services and musical concerts which take place in the Cathedral are broadcast throughout the country on radio and television.

People with hearing aids can now hear services and concerts clearly because a modern loop system transmits sound directly to hearing aids. A standing microphone in the pulpit is linked to carefully placed loudspeakers, and radio microphones are also used for musical events.

Ripon Cathedral has a website of its own, as well as appearing on many other international web pages. The Cathedral clergy, staff and volunteers use email and mobile phones to communicate with people in the community and all around the world.

Even cleaning this magnificent building has changed as new technology has developed. As late as the 1960s, someone remembers cleaning the dust off the floor by covering the nave with barrow loads of wet sand every Monday, so that when he swept the sand up, the dirt would also be collected. Nowadays vacuum cleaners are used, as they are in our homes.

World War I

Ripon and its Cathedral were not physically damaged during either the First or Second World Wars, but many local men and women lost their lives because they were in the armed forces, or other wartime services.

These people have been have been commemorated in the two war memorials. The splendid decorated screen or reredos under the East window was installed four years after the end of the First World War. It has the names of 250 men and one woman who died in service carved into the stone at either side of the ornate statues, which are coloured with paint and gold leaf. Most of these statues are saints who brought Christianity to the North of England. These statues were designed in a similar way to many medieval artworks. They were not meant to look truly lifelike. Instead they are symbolic so that their meaning is easy for

everyone to understand. Across the top of the screen are three large figures, with Christ in the middle. He looks very young, just like many of the men who died in the horrors of the First World War. St George is shown

wearing a tunic with the St George's Cross on it, and is killing a dragon to show that he was a patriotic warrior saint. In contrast, the Archangel Michael looks thoughtful, because he is fighting evil.

There are six other memorials in the Cathedral for men who died in World War I. They remind us of the tragic ways in which young men lost their lives during this war: in the trenches at the Somme, in Flanders and even in an early submarine.

The poet Wilfred Owen visited Ripon Cathedral many times when he was stationed in the local army camp during World War I. He even spent his 25th birthday in the Cathedral, probably reflecting on the horrors of war. Owen became famous for writing poetry which showed the world very clearly how horrifically men were dying in France and Belgium in the trenches of the Western Front. He was killed by a machine gun a week before the end of the war. His mother heard he had died just after the end of the war had been announced.

In 1915 Ripon's population approximately quadrupled in size when the new army camp was built to house 30,000 men. These camps do not all exist anymore, but Ripon Cathedral still hosts special services for the Armed Forces and prayers are said for the local regiment in the Chapel of Justice and Peace, which was consecrated by Dr John Sentamu, the Archbishop of York, in 2006.

World War II

Ripon was not a major target during the second World War, and the Cathedral was not damaged. However, because people were scared that the town might be bombed by the German Air Force, the top of the

Cathedral tower was used for fire-watching, and the oldest pieces of glass in the Cathedral were put down into the Saxon crypt to keep them safe. At the same time, some of the civic treasures which were kept in the town hall were also moved underground for safety. After the war, the pieces of medieval glass were incorporated into the window above the Tudor stone font.

Singing School

Until 1979, all the choirboys or choristers at Ripon Cathedral were boys. Before the choir school was opened in 1960, most of these boys were pupils at nearby schools. One ex-chorister remembers that in the 1950s the boys had to practise singing seven days a week, as well as singing for services, funerals and weddings. Although it was usually enjoyable, he remembers, "As boys you'd get very fidgety. We always used to take comics in and pull them out from under our surplices."

So that the new choir school could be opened in 1960, some valuable old books were sold from the Cathedral library. Two of these were printed by William Caxton on one of England's first printing presses, and were around 500 years old.

The new Cathedral Choir School had strict routines for the singing boys. They had to get up at 6.30am and practise their musical instruments as well as their singing every morning. Then they would go to regular school lessons for the day, followed by more singing rehearsals before they sang for the evening service at 5.30pm. Also, the boys sang for three services on Sundays.

In 1979 girls were allowed to join the choir school and the girls' choir quickly became a success.

1300 Years of St Wilfrid

St Wilfrid is not only important to the Cathedral, but to the city of Ripon. The story of his life is told in the St Wilfrid window, which was installed in 1977. The bright colours and clear shapes still look modern today.

The St Wilfrid parade and service in August continue to this day as a joint celebration for the town and the Cathedral. It involves all sorts of local clubs and organisations dressing up and parading through the town on decorated floats. At the end of the parade, someone dressed as St Wilfrid rides up on a white horse and enters the Cathedral just before a short service begins.

The history of Ripon Cathedral began with St Wilfrid, and his influence is still seen today. In the words of one the Cathedral Welcomers,

"Many pilgrims come, people who travel here far and wide to actually visit the church that St Wilfrid founded."

Times have changed, but Christian worship and the role of the Cathedral within the community of Ripon continues unbroken. A resident describes his view of the Cathedral: "It sits nicely in the centre of the city, a focus, but not aggressive. Nice and warm and comforting."

[Kirsty Hallett]

New low-energy inside and outside lighting was installed at the Cathedral in 2009-10

Activities

1. If you have access to a computer with Internet access, can you find three different photos of Ripon Cathedral?

Can you find the Cathedral website?

2. Walk around the Cathedral:

- How many circular medallions of medieval glass can you see in the window above the Tudor font?

- Which is your favourite of the three Gosney statues?

- Can you find the cushion with pictures from the 20th Century?

St Andrew's crucifixion in medieval glass

3. Design a float for the St Wilfrid parade. Which character would you want to be and what would your costume look like?

4. Imagine you are sitting in the Cathedral while on home leave during World War I. Like Wilfred Owen, write a poem describing your feelings or the things you experienced as a soldier in the trenches.

5. Wordsearch

C	F	S	P	E	A	K	E	R	S
H	R	E	M	O	C	L	E	W	E
A	S	H	O	P	W	H	U	R	Z
I	X	E	N	A	E	B	O	S	N
R	M	A	L	T	B	E	K	I	O
S	E	Y	V	I	S	I	T	O	R
D	L	O	O	P	I	M	S	D	B
R	N	E	H	L	T	I	N	S	O
F	O	N	T	U	E	M	A	I	L
E	N	O	H	P	O	R	C	I	M

14 words are hidden in this grid. They are arranged up, down, forwards, backwards and diagonally. Can you find them all?

BRONZES	CHAIRS
CHOIR	DEAN
EMAIL	FONT
LOOP	MICROPHONE
PULPIT	SHOP
SPEAKERS	VISITOR
WEBSITE	WELCOMER

[Kirsty Hallett]

Participating Ripon Schools

Lists of pupils and staff

Cathedral C of E Primary School
Year 3

Joshua Barthram
Holly Brayshaw
Thomas Clayton
Josh Craggs
Eisladh Finn
Jay Firmin
Joel Gorman
Oliver Haigh
Jodie Harrison
Jessica Hasson
Bethany Hawkyard
Edward Henson
Madison Hobman
Charlotte Howe
Grace Jones
Jemima Lightfoot
Kacey Lund
Shannon Macrae
Hannah McFadden
Josh Mckittrick
Casey-Jade Melville
Phoebe Miller
Susie Morgan
Francesca Quantrill
Chloe Richmond
Lewis Ryder
Charlie Scott
Zeliang Tang
Poppy Williams
Ella Wilson

Teachers: Miss Hardy, Mrs Powell.

_____

Greystone Community Primary School
Year 4

James Atkinson
Grace McConnell
Leanne Ainsley
George Hurry
Charlotte Garrick
Daniel McGarr
Bethany Collard
Nathan Chapman
Mark Gray
Kieran Higginson
Rhiannon Cook
Megan Barton-Clarke
Dion Birch
Chloe Dawson
Charlie Dunn
Jack Goodbarn
Rhys Went

Chloe Dalton
Owen Craft
Daniel Holt
Edward Hoult
Jake Nelson

Teacher: Mrs Lynne Lumsdon.

_____

Holy Trinity C of E Junior School
Year 3

Jessica Herlihy
Lauren Mandelson-Marsh
Myles Hartas
Megan Wallace
Billy Lyman
Daisy Widdowson
Amy Crompton
Lois Wilson
Oliver Cook
Holly Parker

Teachers: Mrs S Scorer, Mrs HM Butterworth.

Participating Schools

Lists of pupils and staff (continued)

**St. Wilfrid's
Catholic Primary
School
Year 6**

Kyle Baldwin
Zach Bateman
Mathew Bell
Joseph Bramley
Joshua Coull
Anna De Martino
Susannah Dinning
Megan Ellis

Darcy Fox
Morgan Gray
Elizabeth Hall
Matthew Hope
Darcy Inchboard
Carlton Jones
Bartek Kurek
Rachel Masterman
Elliot Miller
Amy O'Neill
Jessica Plunkett
Emily Pye
Wiktor Rafinsky

Oliver Simenacz
Joy Sutcliffe
Dana Turner
Elise Whincup

Special contributions
by Kyle, Susannah,
Megan, Darcy.
Emily, Oliver, Joy
and Dana.

Teacher: Maureen
Drought.

Glossary

alabaster	a soft smooth white stone which can be carved easily and looks translucent
alms	gifts of money or food given to the poor
Anglican	Christian (believer in Christ) belonging to the Church of England
Baptism	a service using water as an act of dedication and admission to the Christian Church
Benedictine	a monk who follows the Rule of St Benedict and wears a black habit
bequeath	to leave something to a person in your will
Canon	a priest who is a member of a Cathedral Chapter
casket	a box or chest, often highly decorated
Cassock	a full length garment worn by clergy or choristers
Cathedral	Main church of a diocese where the bishop has his seat
Cavalier	a gentleman with long hair and dressed in fine clothes who supported King Charles I
Celtic Christianity	an ancient form of Christian life and worship
Celts	Irish, Welsh and Scottish tribes who used to live in Britain
Chapter	The governing body (committee) of a Cathedral
Choir	Church singers, also area where they sing– between nave
Choral Offices	daily services sung by priests and choir
Cistercian	a monk who follows strict rules for a simple life and wears a white wool habit
Commonwealth	Government by common agreement of the people or the period when there was no king in England (1649—1660)
Cuddy	a shortened form of Cuthbert
font	a bowl, usually made of stone, which holds water for Baptism
glazier	a person who makes glass, especially for windows

grotesque	a painting or carving of a strange creature, part human, part animal
guestmaster	a monk with the job of welcoming and caring for visitors to a monastery
habit	a monk's full length robe with a hood
illuminated letter	a colourful decorated first letter of a word in a manuscript
incense	a gum which produces a sweet smell when burned, sometimes used in church
indulgence	a certificate excusing a person from any further penance for sins
leper	a person suffering from leprosy, an infectious and contagious disease of skin and nerves
manuscript	a document which is written by hand
mason	a person who carves stone and constructs buildings
Mass	the Service of Eucharist (Communion) in the Catholic Church
medieval	belonging to the Middle Ages (roughly 500—1500 AD)
Minster	An important, originally Saxon, church associated with a monastery
Misericord	a ledge on a seat in a choir stall for leaning on during long services
nave	the main body of a church not including the Choir area
offertory box	a box for collecting money
Parliament	group of people elected or appointed for making or passing laws, a country's government
penance	a penalty for a sin, given by a priest to a person seeking forgiveness
pilgrim	a person who makes a journey to a religious shrine
pilgrimage	a pilgrim's journey

plainsong	unaccompanied church music sung in unison
Prebendal	building or land owned by the Chapter of a Minster or Cathedral
Puritan	Christian emphasising simplicity in worship and a strict lifestyle without frivolity.
Regicide	Someone who kills or shares in the killing of a king
relic	a bone or part of saint's body or an object owned by them, kept as something holy
Ripun	an early spelling of Ripon
Roman Catholic	Christian (believer in Christ) belonging to the Church of Rome
Roundhead	A supporter of Parliament in the time of Charles I, usually with short cropped hair
shrine	a holy place, sometimes holding relics of a saint, and visited by pilgrims for prayer
treaty	important formal agreement between nations
Venerable Bede	a 7th - 8th century Northern monk who wrote about happenings in Anglo-Saxon times
vestments	robes worn by clergy during church services

Afterword by Dean Keith

Well now, dear reader…

Do you feel exhausted after that adventure?

How did it really feel to journey through time with Tilly and Josh?

Did you know, before you read this book, that the Cathedral held so many secrets?

Though it was Tilly and Josh that found the chest and reached into it to find the gold cross and chain, the jewel and the silver longship brooch, I want you to know that there are other things to find in Ripon Cathedral. Perhaps *you* will find one of the animals carved in wood or meet one of the people whose faces appear in the stone. Each of them has a story to tell. Or, perhaps the golden Eagle, who spends his time carrying a big book and watching all the visitors, will speak to you!

What you have to remember is that our beautiful Cathedral has been standing for many hundreds of years. Every day different things have happened both on the inside and on the outside. As Tilly and Josh found out, time never stands still and what they saw and experienced is just a small part of everything that has happened. Ripon Cathedral itself is like a big treasure chest – every time you reach into it you can find something different. Who knows what excitement awaits you?

So, with more adventures to come and more travelling through time to be done, are you ready to be like Tilly and Josh and enjoy the next adventure?